# WARMER
# THAN
# YESTERDAY

Also by Patricia Cleary Miller

*Westport: Missouri's Port of Many Returns*
*Starting a Swan Dive*
*Dresden*
*The Maori Never Age*
*Crimson Lights* (second edition of *The Maori Never Age*)
*Can You Smell the Rain?*

# WARMER
# THAN
# YESTERDAY

NEW & SELECTED POEMS

*Patricia Cleary Miller*

*with a foreword by Desmond Egan*

BkMk Press
Kansas City, Missouri

BkMk Press, Inc.
bkmkpress.org
Fine books since 1971
bkmkpress.org

Author photo: Marianne Kilroy

Cover photo: Copyright © Ashmolean Museum, University of Oxford. Reprinted by permission. This image does not reflect a current exhibit of the museum.

Editor, book design: Ben Furnish

Library of Congress Cataloging-in-Publication Data

Names: Miller, Patricia Cleary, author. | Egan,  Desmond , writer of
    foreword.
Title: Warmer than yesterday : new & selected poems / Patricia Cleary
    Miller ; with a foreword by Desmond Egan.
Description: Kansas City, Missouri : BkMk Press, [2024] | Summary: "The
    voices in Patricia Cleary Miller's Warmer Than Yesterday: New and
    Selected Poems struggle with four of life's greatest confusions: home,
    war, death, and love. With humor, pathos, and ambiguity-after all, today
    is warmer than yesterday-they savor their experiences even if they never
    seem to find out all the answers as they search in Kansas City and all
    over the world. This book highlights new poems as well as work from her
    numerous books spanning over thirty years"-- Provided by publisher.
Identifiers: LCCN 2024036268 | ISBN 9781943491407 (trade paperback)
Subjects: LCGFT: Poetry.
Classification: LCC PS3563.I4194 W37 2024 | DDC 811/.54--dc23/
eng/20240812
LC record available at https://lccn.loc.gov/2024036268

## Contents

Section III: Near Death

Section IV: Near Love

To the Clearys: Cathy, John, Joanie

## Foreword

The great Irish poet, Patrick Kavanagh, once wrote,
> *What wisdom's ours*
> *If such there be*
> *Is a flavour of personality.*

I agree and always look for it in a poetry collection. *Warmer Than Yesterday* certainly passes the test with flying colours. It is full of the personality of Patricia Cleary Miller: generous, witty, engaged, cosmopolitan, female and, most important of all, compassionate.

It is indeed a truly female voice, with real insight into the condition of women, from her persona "Mother" (who features quite a lot but always to some purpose) to that of younger and young females and— delightfully—to her own, about which she is clear-eyed, honest, and knowing. This womanly quality, so notable in her last collection, is everywhere in evidence here. She brings that delicate eye for detail to everything she writes about, be it clothes, colours (*a green moiré hallway*), plants (*larkspur in the craters*) or people (*giggling in church*). This quality makes her descriptions vivid and immediate, like the plywood which covers the windows of an abandoned house.

The range is wide, from love (a constant theme) to war (e.g. the dead Kurdish baby), to sculpture (mostly). What I like especially is the sense of humour which is so delightfully there: *Deer Crossing but No deer*, or the youthful road of possibilities,
> *Perhaps it leads to Italy.*

or the reaction of different groups of soldiers to works of art. That last, a highlight.

Sometimes the author's reporter's eye can lead her into anecdotage: a few of the poems seem to have strayed from a better-fitting short story format—but what seems occasionally too close to the prosaic can suddenly lift into memorable, poetry,
> *Guests fade into the midnight street, laughter dies away*

I know that feeling!

I certainly recommend *Warmer Than Yesterday*: read it gradually and you will not only enjoy the quality and the vision of its enjoyably quirky author—but also learn something of the female experience in the world we all share.

—Desmond Egan
County Kildare, Ireland, June 2024

## *We Never Thought of Aristotle*

I watched him undress. Slender, firm.
Lithe and smooth, he was a work of art,
a Renaissance sculture, marble or bronze,
like Donatello's two young Davids in the Bargelo.
Or like what Eleanor of Aquitaine said of her Henry—
he came at her with a mind like Aristotle
and a form like mortal sin.

The mortal sin we don't discuss.
You can imagine the breathing and writhing,
I will remember our stroking, caressing.
We could have danced on the hillsides,
weaving flowers into our hair.
We never thought of Aristotle.

# I
*Near Home*

## I Ask the Little Prince about Yellow Roses

*If you love a flower that lives on a star, it is sweet to look at the sky at night.*
*All the stars are abloom with flowers.* —Antoine de Saint Exupéry, *The Little Prince*

Can the flower bloom in the desert?
How does it?
With her four thorns, can she defend herself
against the blazing sun?
Too much
not enough
rain.

Must there be color?
Can black and white film show a flower
if the flower is white?

If you snarl at a flower
will it wither and crumble?

Only one bouquet per room now.
Long-stemmed yellow roses at dinner.

Why breed roses for color alone?
We must have perfume
in every room
and in the garden
and in the woods
and in the stars.

## Mother Is Scrubbing Her Floors

Mother is scrubbing her floors, she won't use a mop;
she scrubs on her hands and her knees with a brush,
she says she gets the corners, she says she does not slop the baseboards,
she says it's cooler down here, she says it tightens her thighs.

Mother is polishing her silver and brass;
with a toothbrush she is scrubbing her great grandmother's cut crystal,
she is carrying baskets and trays of heavy objets d'art
down to the kitchen to soak in ammonia;
she is climbing on ladders to wash Chinese vases,
she says it's aerobic, she says Dad can take back the treadmill.

Mother is mending and washing and ironing;
she is ironing Dad's handkerchiefs, his shirts and his shorts.
On her knees beside the clawfoot bathtub she is scrubbing
her great grandmother's table cloths, her napkins as large as bridge cloths.
With her yellow-gloved finger she traces the monogram, Patrick O'Rourke;
she boasts, *One hundred years old and never been starched;*
*look: no tears, no holes; still so stiff they could stand up by themselves.*

Mother strides from room to room opening or closing the draperies,
turning the lamps on or off, watching the light
dance on, caress her furniture, her silver and brass and cut crystal,
memorizing the contents of closets,
tracing her ancestors' trips to China and Egypt and Russia.

*Mother Remembers Flowers*

Not flowers, really. She never planted anything in her life.
She thinks flowers come in a long box tied with a silk ribbon,
or else already arranged in a lavender crystal vase.
She would be horrified were I to inform her that
in order to have a flower garden she
would need to get down on her knees and dig in the dirt.

What Mother remembers are corsages.
She says she received a lot of them
and always pressed them in a great big book,
until the spine broke and she had to find another book.
She said it was the family Bible.
Now I know this is not true because she grew up Catholic

and they never had a family Bible.
She has a tiny gold-edged green leather Bible by her bed,
but I can tell she has never opened it.

Still, she remembers her corsages.
She says that she received so many that
once a week she set aside time to care for them.
She unwrapped the narrow ribbons,
peeled off the green tape, pulled out the green wires,
and smashed the blooms as flat as she could
onto a paper towel with the heel of her hand.
Then she found a page in the Bible with a nice illustration;
in pencil at the top of the page she noted
the name of the boy and the date and the occasion;
then she laid the smashed flower on the illustration,
closed the book firmly, and sat on it for a few minutes.

The nice ribbons she saved for her hair;
the ordinary ones she rolled up and stored in her top drawer.
She inserted the pearl-headed pins into her
great aunt's embroidered pincushion.
She still has the pins, and there are a lot of them.
But I have never found a single dried flower
in any book, large or small.

## Mother Mourns

Mother is mourning the end of summer.
She is saying goodbye to her white linen skirts.
She is saying goodbye to her pastel flowered sundresses.
She thought she could wear her dark cottons
just a few more times with a sweater or shawl.
She gave up bread and pasta and sugary tea all summer,
hoping to fit in to her tight white jeans by August.
And now in October she feels doomed and fat.

She refuses to zip up the garment bags,
to close the door to the storage closet,
to *entomb and forget.*
She hopes for more warm sunny days.
She says her new silk cream-colored pants are winter white;
she wants to remember to wear them
when that warm day comes at Thanksgiving.

She refuses to turn on the furnace  It's too soon.
She sits in her cold dark house wrapped in a silk summer shawl.
The leaves turn gold and orange,
but she still yearns for pink and turquoise.
Halloween decorations cry out from the attic,
but she holds on to the forsythia wreath, to the lavender garland.

We need to bring the tropical plants inside.
She asks, *Isn't it going to be eighty degrees over the weekend?*
She plugs in the space heater in the sunroom and stares out the windows.

I try to remind her, *Remember how you hate the summer heat?*
*Remember your dozen cashmere sweaters in jewel tones?*
*The sparkly Saint John knit you got at the store closing?*
*Your shoes and tights and big gold jewelry?*
*Haven't you missed them all summer?*

She says, *Eight months until I see my white linen skirts again.*
*Will they fit me?  Will I live until then?*
*The summer flew by and I didn't even wear all my clothes.*

## Silk and Velvet Walls

Each room is different: bittersweet velvet drawing room—
not orange, not red, a Chinese palace color;
green silk moiré hallway, the tint of shadows on grass;
dining room wallpaper—elephants amble along the Ganges,
golden thrones on their backs, against palm trees, against blue sky;
soft puppy-brown bedroom; tortoise-shell bathroom;
celadon silk dressing room.

And everywhere ormolu wall sconces, sterling silver objets,
Baroque picture frames; a marble bust of Ptolemy,
charging bronze horses.

I see only colors, can't hear anything:
the padded velvet and silk silence the rooms.
Guests fade into the midnight street, laughter dies away.

Servants gather linen napkins, crystal champagne flutes
from silver tables, extinguish the ormolu wall sconces.
Bittersweet velvet fades to gray, the dining room elephants
pavanne in silence beneath palm trees and along the river,
as light from the street seeps through ivory silk curtains.

The master walks slowly down his green moiré hallway
into his soft brown bedroom. All is quiet.

By the time the house catches fire,
he is long dead.
His Louis XVI treasures have been auctioned off.

The roof caves in, the snow falls.
Now tarps still blanket the roof,
plywood still covers the windows.
Inside is darkness.

In the garden, trumpet vines envelope the topiaries,
obscure the lap-pool, choke the espaliered fruit trees.

## Bench Is Not on Firm Ground

Madge Hall's Garden: Estate Sales by Mr. Nova

### I.

Tall bamboo slumps in the lily pond.
Just a few lily pads, no blooms,
still float among the rowing bugs.
Aquamarine paint cracks, rusts
at the waterline. A concrete Saint Francis, headless,
stands on a white tin table in a puddle
of thick rust. Someone has put the saint's
severed head in the basket he carries at his side
for giving loaves and fishes to the poor.

*Granite stone bench 9'7" long as is*
*$3500. Please do not sit back*
*because bench is not on firm ground.*
Squirrels have scattered walnut shells
on all the benches, and my skirt is white.

### II.

With other women in flowered silk gowns,
men in bright linen jackets, white shoes,
I wander the garden paths seeking
a place to sit. We bear in our hands,
like gifts from the Magi, our Sèvres and Limoges
dinner plates heaped with ham, fruit, hot
sweet mustard sauce; under the wisteria
arbor, over the mandala-patterned
walkways. At every turn, a new wonder:
wide-mouthed lions shoulder a curved bench,
maidens caress laughing infants.
Moonlight filters through locust and elm trees,
augments the glow from the Georgian house
and from dozens of votive candles hidden
in the foliage. Reflections dance
in the fishponds, against Doric columns,
curl around cupids in fountains,
around holly bushes, over lace
tablecloths, spark back from diamond jewelry.

III.
*European 19th cent. iron*
*Double basin-fountain 99" high*
*as is $10,000.*

*No problem getting it out of here,*
Mr. Nova tells a dealer from New York.
She never had to countersink:
own weight holds it in place.
Water from cupid's cornucopia.
Plugged in now. Runs perfectly.

An old lady in taupe slacks, wearing a
rosary as jewelry, puts Saint Francis'
head back on his neck. I'm afraid
the head will roll off and break on the bricks;
I put the head back in the basket.

*Francis I Early 16th c.*
*Marble well as is $3000*

*7 doric granet columns*
*81" high*

One hundred windows of a ten-story condo
building spy on Madge's garden.
In its parking lot, new BMW's push
against Madge Hall's Italian iron fencing.
*Fencing not for sale*

IV.
Late that night
all the fencing
was stolen

## Jennie Butchart's Gardens

One gray day in 1904 Jennie Butchart looked out over her husband's dying Portland
Cement quarry on Vancouver Island and envisioned a Paradise. At seaside, Isaburo
Kishida designed The Japanese Garden. Jennie had tons of topsoil carted in from
the neighboring farmland, created The Sunken Garden; friends brought plants that
she stuffed into the rocks: she hung from a bosun's basket. She converted the tennis
courts into The Italian Garden. Butler Sturtevant transformed the kitchen garden
into The Rose Garden. Now 1.3 million people a year visit the fifty-five acre paradise.


I. *1904. Jennie Butchart Speaks*
Cold and desolate the sea, ashen the cliffs,
crumbling the dead gray quarry, empty the caves.
Ash and dust cover the cedars, mist out to the sea.
Far away my English forests and rolling hills,
far away my family, my childhood home.


II. *2009. A Visitor Speaks.*
Flowers burst like fireworks, colors explode.
Lombardy poplars and Persian Plums disguise, obliterate the quarry,
vestigial old smokestack surveys
spring—pansies, forget-me-nots, tulips, daisies;
summer—rhododendron, blooming cherry and plum trees.


At home, my garden grows green.
Every shade of green. Everything grows.
But I'm not Jennie: I do not know the names of anything.
My elm trees may be dead, but the vines are lush.
Something nameless will soon engulf the garage.
In the bed of English ivy where I planted bulbs last fall—
dozens of tulips and daffodils—sprout blighted blooms;
now Jack-in-the-beanstalk vines shoot up.
Adam and Eve need to come along with their clipping shears.
Jennie Butchart needs to come with her Japanese and German designers.


I would like to call out,
> *Oh, Raimondo, could you please plant an oak tree here,*
> *a magnolia there? Spirea, forsythia?*
> *I would like a euonymus hedge on the west,*
> *a topiary grouping in front.*
> *Could you please cut those peonies*
> *and arrange them in my grandmother's cut crystal vases?*

## Queen Nefertari's Knees

Wrapped and wrapped in fine linen strips, now black,
black bones protruding, Nefertari's legs, just part of her legs,
all that remains of her mummy:
the video shows them floating
in the lowest chamber of her tomb
looted long ago in the Valley of the Queens,
wrapped and wrapped in fine linen strips,
now black, black bones protruding.
The most loved wife of Ramses II.

The day after each Christmas I iron
Great Grandmama O'Rourke's linen napkins,
big as bridge tablecloths, stiff and white;
stiff as though starched, so white they never need bleach.
One hundred years old.  How long did she have them?
How often did she use them? Who ironed them for her?
I could cut them into strips, freshen Nefertari's knees.

*Juxtapositions: On Watching Clark Gable in* Mogambo

I hate mosquito netting. It separates people.
On safari, take your pills at the same time every day.
Drink gin and tonic. Tsetse flies love blue and black.
Cover your face with a white bandanna.

Zebra and wildebeest thunder across the plain,
a hippo looms out of the swamp, lunges, mouth opens;
subsides, lumbers back. A panther leaps at Grace Kelly.
Clark Gable whistles and a thousand flamingoes flap
into flight, darken the sky against the lowered sun.

Chest-pounding gorilla, high in a tree, drumbeat
louder louder, cries and shouts; young ones
eating pineapples, tumbling in the weeds. One male charging
fast, right at Clark Gable. Now two huge males
braying huffing charging. In an instant, they all turn
and run back into, disappear into, the brush; three babies leap behind.
We'll return tomorrow to capture a baby for the Chicago zoo.

> My little sister, afraid of bugs, screamed
> that the moths crashing our window screens would tangle
> in her hair. I had to kill the moths and spiders,
> so Cathy wouldn't shriek, so Mommy would not
> charge in  and confiscate our flashlights.

> Cicadas, loud every evening, just at bedtime.
> Gray-brown shells climbed the tree trunks every
> morning. We collected them in Easter baskets,
> painted them with watercolors, made earrings, brooches, necklaces.
> On our limestone walls we found fossils: white sea worms,
> dinosaur wings. In the creek bed we found smooth
> dark rocks. With our few crayons we colored our cache,
> tried not to break those crayons or wear them down.
> then hawked our treasures. Who ever bought those shiny objects?

Clark Gable ignites a stick with embers from the campfire,
lights his cigarette with the flaming brand.
Leopard strolls into Ava Gardner's tent, turns and leaves. No sound.
Tomorrow drums will lure the gorillas into the clearing.
> No cicadas this year. Quiet evenings. Just a light breeze.
> And the helicopters. No fires yet. No drums here.

## They Said They Were Picky Birds

As toddlers, my brother and sister ran around
the yard in widening or narrowing circles
chanting *Having fun, having lots of fun.*
They rolled in the grass like puppies,
singing, their voices high and squeaky.
They called themselves *Picky Birds,*
so we did too.
We pondered; they didn't explain.
Was it their singing? Their hopping around?
They were cute and we did not ask too much.
One day they piped up:
*Picky Birds pick flowers and they have orange hair.*
Their answer did not answer.
We didn't understand, but they kept the name.

Then we saw them toss their troll dolls into the air,
play catch like baby leprechauns,
snatch the heads off dandelions.
Mother floated their golden offerings in juice glasses.

## They Yelled It Staccato

*You're not one bit funny and you're not one bit cute.*
I knew I was in trouble as I ran away
laughing, climbed up high into Mrs. Moseley's
huge magnolia tree, always in flower,
gooey, fragrant. Granny could not see me,
she kept shaking her wooden spoon at the back yard.

*You're not one bit funny and you're not one bit cute,*
Grandpa yelled at my cute little sister
as she cut star-shaped holes in the black-out curtains
with Aunt Jane's cuticle scissors, during the air raid.

*You're not one bit funny and you're not one bit cute,*
Mommy yelled at my cute little brother
when he flushed his green squirt gun down the toilet
of our historic house, historic plumbing.

They yelled it staccato, like clapping, like marching.
Like giggling in church, breaths pulsing
fast as our feet could carry us,
down the stairs, out the door,
around the house, up the tree.
Never caught.

## Boy on Crutches

Frederick and I were reading by the fire in the library.
I saw Ellen, about 14, in the hall, with a boy on crutches.
His legs dangled, did not seem to have any bones.
I saw her take the big bottle of Christmas brandy
from the liquor cabinet.  I heard the stair glide going up.

I followed the two of them up to the second floor.
Down the hallway he lurched on his crutches,
thrust his dangling legs forward in no steady rhythm.
It took a long time for him to climb to the third floor,
and Ellen kept pushing him from behind, and I kept calling out
*What do you think you are doing?*
And *What is your name, young man?*

They climb out onto the flat roof.
I hear them scrambling up the steep slope
to the tippy-top "widow's walk."
I call up, *Come down* and *Stop it right now.*
They snigger, like thick glass breaking.

I run back down to Frederick in the library, tell him,
*Ellen is on the roof with a boy on crutches*
*and your big bottle of Christmas brandy.*
He yawns, *I don't see any boy on crutches.*
*What are you talking about?*

I run out into the garden, call up to the tippy-top roof.
Ellen and the boy are laughing in the moonlight,
shadowed by tall swaying tree limbs.
They keep on giggling and guffawing.
I tell Frederick.  He yawns, *I don't see anything.*

## Baby Squirrel

Strolling up the hill at twilight, I heard chanting.

I.
*Baby Squirrel, Baby Squirrel,*
the three boys chanted: jumped up and down
in the middle of the road, held onto their bikes,
laughed, danced around each other,
*Baby Squirrel, Baby Squirrel.*
Three skinny teenagers; the youngest one
pulled at his gray sweatpants, grabbed his pants leg
and swooped up by its neck scruff
a baby squirrel—downy gray, dove soft,
small as an Easter chick—held it
gently aloft as would its own mother.

*Ooohs* and *Aaahs.*
Then: *Tate, Put it down!*
And—*I want to take him home.*
—*Tate, you can't.*
—*It needs its mother.*
—*Where is its mother?*
The three boys insisting,
three mono choruses, circling, chanting
*Baby Squirrel, Baby Squirrel.*

Motherly, I joined the chorus:
—*Put him down. Put him in the bushes.*
*Maybe its mother will find him*
*before the cats or foxes.*
Tate lowered the squirrel into the peonies.

It jumped up onto the rock wall,
jumped down into the grass, ran into
the street, crossed the street, more grass;
another rock wall, jumped up, down,
skirted along the sidewalk, feinted at my shoe,
jumped at Tate. Tate picked him up,
cradled him inside his jacket.
It squeaked like a toy mouse.

*—I want to take him home.*
*—Tate, you can't.*
*—Where is its mother?*
Tate lowered the squirrel to the grass.

It scooted toward me—
I stroked its tiny head,
and it dashed on up the road,
like teenaged Jesus tricking his parents
and going off with God only knows,
avoiding all foxes and bandits,
getting home eventually.

II.
*Good evening, Gentlemen*, I said to the boys.
*The sun is setting. You are far from home,*
*you need to hurry to get there before dark.*
As the boys rode on up the hill,
two big white cars drove up to me,
two matrons in each.
*—Are you all right Ma'am?*
*We've been watching you with those boys.*
*We circled back. Are you all right?*
I said—*They remind me of my students. I miss them.*

## Dancing Lady at the Luggage Repair

Who are you, Bill-Robinson-Feet Lady tap tap?
Leather mini-skirt tap tap ta dum dum dum,
purple turtleneck, purple hose, knee-length
thick purple scarf, tap tap ta dum dum dum—
With that carapace, you're a purple Venus.
Your white curls turn pink tap tap.
Who are you thinking of, who will you meet
with your once-the-latest Samsonite
shiny smooth weekender? Tadum,
twirl feet, Fred Astaire, just don't let
the dancing master steal your jewelry,
does he have a jacuzzi?
Jerk hands at the wrists, shake head
side to side, back; eyes front,
whom do you see, not me, where's the clerk?
Feet slide out—back—in,
ice skates, roller blades. Do your children
grandchildren know tap tap ta dum?
Mouth open breathe in, head bob up and down.
He's on the train, the boat, do you need him?
Who could keep up with you, Lady?
You'll soar up over the moon,
tap ta tap tap tap ta tum.

*Cataracts*
Written while healing from eye surgery

*A. Mahakala*
I.
I wanted to be an iridescent butterfly
with wings like reflections of Chartres windows on the sunny
pavement—not the bright dark glass itself,
but the gossamer pastel shadows.  Mother disagreed,

spoke of the whim of the wind, of evanescence.
She did not want to be a butterfly:
my lovely Titian-haired mother, my slender mother
of many wiggly children.  She said she wanted

to be a cow: to sit quietly cared for,
comfortably eating alone in the shade,
useful but unmolested.

II.
Mahakala, the bodhisattva of
our clan, wears a Black Coat.  He roars at the
evil spirits, all the bacteria
and viruses, all the bad blond young men,

the handsome seducers, the evil ones who steal
innocence and treasure.  We need a ferocious
protector; I want a calm comforting lady,
but Mahakala is a fighter.  I want

a quiet grandfather God in a long white robe.
I do not want the piercing light, the burning
bush, the whirlwind.  I do not want razor
claws, blazing swords.  Please Mahakala,

Saint Michael, gods on horseback: while you are out
smiting and pillaging microbes and parasites,

please leave with me a quiet Comforter;
please lay me down beside still waters,
in the shade.

*B. God Is in All Sparkly Things*
I.
Quiet here, end of the hall.
Outside, the sun shines,
but we sit in the dark.
Morphine, phenergan, potassium chloride,
keep her comfortable.
Spinal meningitis—viral or bacterial?
Until the test results,
they are keeping her comfortable.

> She says, *God is in all sparkly things—*
> *in rainbows, stars, sun, water, diamonds, waterfalls;*
> *God is in puppies, sushi, chocolate, grandfathers.*

The air conditioning is not working.
So many cell phones, ringing all at once.
Sick father, screaming grandson,
screaming and kicking for hours.

Her head throbs, she cannot turn.  She moans.
Her face is gray. She vomits. She holds
her rosary, her blond hair fluffs around her face.
I stroke her arm, her mother rubs her feet.
Will she die?

Tests inconclusive.  Tests contradictory.
Doctor away.  Insurance ambiguous.
She is not comfortable.  The morphine drips.

*Where is God when there is so much frantic worry?*
*Is God in the frantic worry?  Does God control the breathing?*

II.
The generations clash—the elders forget their wild youth,
the middle ones continue their free days.
> *Stay at the party and dance wildly,*
> *just do not leave with the handsome stranger.*

Is God in common sense?
Does God protect the raped girl from death?

III.
They were dancing, drinking, laughing.
She remembers his car, the top down,
the wind whipping her golden hair;
she remembers his sparkling
blue eyes, *like heavenly jewels.*

She remembers waking up in his bed;
does not remember how she got home.

Later she did not understand the pain,
the blisters. Never considered she might
be pregnant. She could not turn
her head, walk across the room.

IV.
Of what worth are propriety, morality,
rules of grandmothers, of churches?
What imports is safety: you must stay alive.
You must live. Live.

Was I that naïve? Was my mother wild?
Which girls are not wild?
Where is God? Please protect this child.

> She says her angel wears a sparkly pink dress;
> crystals crown her white-blond hair,
> cascading like Botticelli's Venus's hair.
> The angel's wings *shoot out of her back*
> *when she needs to fly.*

Morphine drips.  Her head throbs.
We stroke her arm, massage her feet.
Who sees the angel? Who sees God?

*C. Who Walks in My Garden in July?*
Day lilies promise tangerine and pink,
mandevilla almost blooms, lilac grows tall,
but spindly, no buds. Hibiscus forced into iron lattice

refuses to flourish. Buds thirst. Clot, knot. Shrivel. Vines twine

rusting frame, loop, twist. Virginia creeper, trumpet
vines, nameless vines: blanket the coreopsis,
clematis, columbine; snake under mint, encircle
Italian terra cotta pots, wrap the fence,

strangle the lilac. Costly perennials guaranteed
to shoot up two feet, wither. Weeds masquerade, flaunt.
Sylphs desert the butterfly plant; gnomes tunnel
too deep; salamanders dismiss the burning bush,

hide in damp logs; undines desiccate like salted slugs.
Night deluge, day desert, summer sirocco.  Damp dry chalky earth.

D. Caitlin's Angel
Caitlin says, *My angel's name is Alexis.*
*She has porcelain skin and vibrant green eyes;*
*and light pink fingernails and toenails like me.*
*Her dress is translucent silky pink with sparkly swirls.*

*Crystals crown her white-blond hair, cascading like*
*Botticelli's Venus's hair. Her wings, light pink*
*with crystals, shoot out of her back when she needs to fly.*
*She protects me.* Caitlin holds her rosary,

her pale blond hair fluffs around her face.
Her face is gray. If she moves, her head throbs
and she vomits. I stroke her arm, her mother keeps
a cold cloth on her forehead. The first nurse

missed her vein. Morphine drips. The boyfriend
rubs her feet. Who sees Alexis? God?

*First and Last*

*Helen Gladden Twiss— last breath; Alice Twiss—first steps:*
*her grandfather, Washington Gladden, speaks.*


Last week Baby Alice was crawling
on the Turkey carpet, scooching in circles,
bouncing back and forth on her hands and knees.

Today she stands in the doorway to her mother's room,
squeals at me, holds out her arms, laughing.
She wobbles, pushes one foot forward, lurches.
Little white shoes. The other foot out, wobbles.
Long white dress, lacy panels. Pushes
her foot out, lurches. Lacy cap, embroidered
pink flowers, strawberry curls, shoe button eyes.
Her first steps. She keeps on, laughing, holding
out her arms. I rush toward her, scoop her up,
swing her over my head, laughing laughing.

When I arrived at the house just now George said
Helen was a little better, she was breathing steadily,
quietly. He thought her fever would break soon.
Suffused with hope for his sweet young wife.

It is the end of the third week.
I know the symptoms, the progression,
from the War, from Prince Albert.
Still, most sufferers do not die.
Jenny has been tending our daughter these two weeks.

Helen coughs in the next room.
George says *come quickly,*
takes Baby from my arms.

I sit in the chair by Helen's bed.
She coughs and rasps.
She smiles at me, moves her lips.
Her eyes flutter shut, then open.
She closes her eyes.
Breathes hard, stops.
One long final exhalation.
Baby coos in the hallway.

## Praise Him

At Saint Joseph's Trappist Abbey

The moon-faced tower
behind me scraped the dull sky.
I walked up the hill

through old snow still white,
iced, dusk-gleaming, over swift-
snagged gun-blue river,

on cracked macadam,
to pale sun sliding behind
low stone arches, bell
tower, chapel.  Ostracized
behind visitors wall, old

pilgrim lost in a
thicket, motherless child, I
closed my eyes against

the dark.  Above me,
one electric light and the
thought—*Keep to your path:*

*love whom I send you.*
*Write what I tell you.  Dance what*
*I show you.  Thank Me.*

## Chris Norman, Small Bagpipes

Chris Norman, small bagpipes green velvet,
drone, low drone, whine, start melody,
stomp heel, stomp terrazzo floor—

Cynthia taps her fingers, claps her hands,
Chinese silk dress, Cynthia drums
fingers on red silk skirt,
pianos her long fingers on red skirt,
drums faster taps faster,
everyone vibrating stomping
Ellen's face is aglow and Rick is bobbing
his head up and down and
electric currents pulse out the top of my head.

These Celts are my ancestors,
They danced on the highlands,
Mother's hair was red and she danced on the hills,
electricity sparks out the top of my head,
Cynthia tapping tapping,
my auburn-haired mother dances on the hills.

Not Cromwell, but Bonnie Prince Charlie—
Thomas Kelton: down up the hill, feint.
Mayhem.  Surrounded. Captured.
Deported.  Many died on the ship
to Lynn, Massachusetts iron works.
Oh please, my Celtic ancestor, live
long enough to reproduce.

Cynthia keeps clapping and Ellen's face is aglow,
and Rick is bobbing his head up and down,
and we are all tapping and tapping and stomping
and drinking single malt with nary a splash of water,
and we are all stomping and tapping and
Chris looks mesmerized and everyone has gone into a reverie.

Oh Mother with red hair,
where are you now?
Please oh please be dancing on the highlands.

Mother why did you cut your hair,
dye it black?
        Why did you die?

## Now, After All

Listen to the tree frogs
                    in the moonlight.
Don't make a sound
                    now.

Locusts buzz, tree frogs chirp
                    in the night breeze.
It will be over soon
                    now.

A truck shifts gears
                    in the moonlight.
It doesn't hurt that much
                    now.

Hum. Stop. A small plane
                    in the night breeze.
You go numb
                    now.

Your legs out straight
                    in the moonlight.
You asked for it
                    after all.

Your arm out stiff
                    in the night breeze.
No one will ever know
                    after all.

Your hand a new moon
                    in the moonlight.
You'll forget
                    after all.

## Mother Keeps Turning off the Lights

Mother keeps turning off the lights.
Every time she leaves a room.
The minute the sun goes down.
The whole house looks haunted.
Shadows from the streetlights.

She bumps into furniture,
fans her arms out,
hits the bed's four posters,
the bathroom door.

She says her cataract surgery worked fine,
her eyes adjust to the dark.
Pretty quickly.
The light from the street keeps her safe.
She is getting the light bill under control.

     I can't see.
     Everything is shadows.
     Why doesn't she turn on the lights?

     My eyes are bad.
     Monthly shots don't really help,
     they just delay the inevitable.

     Why doesn't she turn on the lights?
     She can afford it.
     I hate to visit.
     She is just trying to annoy me.
     To drive me away.

# II
## *Near War*

## Kurdish Baby, Her Bath

Iraq, April 1991

She could be an alabaster statue,
cool, smooth, slippery as soap.
She could warm to my touch,
curve her limbs, relax in the water.

Her arms could float out, her legs bend,
she could wiggle her toes, kick, splash;
open her eyes, and they would be blue,
she would see me and smile,
her hair curling around her face.

I sit her on my lap.  She trembles
pale with cold, her lips are blue.
I wrap her in a towel, soft
thick, rub her in the towel

and her skin turns pink.
I hold her so she stands.
Here is her dress, her hair ribbon,
her shoes, her dolly.

Here is warm milk, bread, jam.
She sits on my lap
and I sing to her
my child my grandchild,

why are you
an alabaster statue,
why translucent?

A young man in a red sweater
props up a corrugated barricade,
small boys stare over it.
Sheltered, three black-cloaked women
hunch like buffalo, sharp-boned,
wash you in a tin basin.

Snow melts in their hands,
red hands, wide as flounder,

43

supple as trout, dough-kneading,
baggage-lugging, tent-hoisting;
slender fingers that can teach
a newborn's lips to nurse.

My milk dried,
she drank sugared snow-water.
Rub snow over alabaster,
caress, polish with flowered
towel, red-streaked.

One eye is slightly open,
upper lip still soft pink.
A red mark on her forehead.

I dry her with the towel,
wrap her in my lavender print scarf,
swaddle her with white ribbons, pretty bows.

With his pickax Abdullah Ahmed
attacks the rocky soil.
I lay her in the hole.

It will fill with water,
snow will cover her,
flowers may grow,

and she will become mountain
snow, water, lilacs,
my alabaster vase.

Saddam Hussein will not win,
Turkey will let us off this mountain.
American helicopters drop flour, blankets.

*Rice*

for Judith Thompson and Arn Chorn

I bend over, pick the rice, rice is good,
I eat rice, bend over, pick the rice pick plop
rice sticks in water in light my face in water
rice is good, rice sticks, rice sticky,
Mother Father I pick, steam, eat rice.
Buddha's soft face, my face in the water.
Mother Father Buddha eat rice.

I give Him my bowl, my pomegranate,
the jewels of the Lord God Buddha dance on the water.
I am a drop of water in the sea in Buddha I am water,
I dip my hand in and out of water, hold the sunlight
hold the jewels of rice and water and light,
the heart of light, palm fronds, coconut, date,
waxy leaves, sparkling lizards, rice

Mekong, Yangtze, Ganges, Tigris, Euphrates, Mississippi
rice, corn, beans, peanuts, tobacco, sugar palm, salt.
Sandstone Buddhas.
My fields are prey to Siam.  Annam.
France.  Japan.  Viet Nam.  Pol Pot.
A club misses my head, Mother slips in water
blood in water, water bugs in light

Father shot in green leaves,
Uncles Brothers dragged from hut,
Sisters Aunts starve slowly in the sunlight,
bullets skim my chest.
Bayonets rip my body, soldiers eat
my kidneys one after the other
while I still live.

Sandstone columns lurch,
Buddha topples.
The Lord God splinters,
shatters on red tiles,
children's wails
claw my temple walls.
Stars rise like jewels.

*Jersey Shore, 1943*

Mother was very aware of fashions.
Her bathing suit was shiny white.
When I was about three she bought me
a red wool bikini with big white polka dots.
It was scratchy. The color ran and faded.
I was the first toddler to wear a bikini.

At Granny and Grandpa's beach house
I skipped back and forth on the hard sand.
Just off the shore, periscopes
of German U-Boats.

> No, it could not have been a bikini
> because it was still during the war,
> and the bikini was not until later
> when the French man invented it,
> *small and explosive, like the bomb,*
> he would say.

Still, it had a bare midriff.
The wool was scratchy, but I was very cute.

I ran back and forth on the hard sand. Mother splashed
her feet in the foam, cuddling Baby Sister.
Granny and Aunt Jane strolled along.

Undulating on the sand a big blob of bubble,
big as my head, shiny like the sky,
rainbow colors.  Iridescent. I picked it up.

Fire in my hand. Dropped it fast.
Fire on my leg, slippery and burning,
licking my leg.

I screamed. Mother screamed,
thrust the baby at Granny, fast,
scooped me up and ran into the ocean.
I saw the U-Boat periscopes.
The sea water stung, I kept on screaming.

Back at Granny's house, when I pushed my bathing suit
bottoms down my tummy was white and cold.
My leg was red but it did not hurt any more.
Mother let me dress myself. She was feeding the baby.

## What Does It Rain?

I
Rain all week.
Today no rain, but water just sits
under the grass, even in the flowerpots.
All our roofs are wet.

Jack, my dad, climbs his scaffolding
up to his roof.  He scrapes old paint and
wood rot off the west dormer.
I glance up. A little pinkish orange line,
flickering, moving fast, east to west.
Jack yells *Get a hose.*
The line is moving north to south,
along the edge of the dormer.
Jack yelling *Get a hose. Get a hose.*

I grab my hose, shoot water at Jack's roof.
Orange spikes, red spikes moving fast.
Hose too short, flames,
Jack yells *Get a hose. Get a hose.*

Water still sits under the grass, in the flowerpots.

II.
One plane is called YoYo—*it always comes back.*
In the infantry there are bodies,
but the planes go away and don't come back.
B-17 bomber, flying fortress, 9 machine guns; big, loud.
*You do not want to get into that airplane.*
*You get in because your friends are getting in.*
Norden bomb sight:  *Drop a bomb in a pickle barrel from 20,000 feet.*
Hamburg. Nantes. Regensburg. Schweinfurt ball-bearing plant.
*Not a dog or a cat survived, but the target remained intact.*
Mustang escorts hold back, Luftwaffe attack, flak.
B-17 bombers don't come back. We have no bodies.

III.
Bill is making his plans.
His friend owns a funeral home. He says
*You have no idea how hot the furnace.*

IV.
Okinawa was a rain of steel, a typhoon of steel.

My brother says *From Tinian, 600 B-29s would take off,*
*wing to wing, every thirty seconds;*
*two hours for all to get airborne.*
They rained down fire day and night.  Weeks.  Months.
Tokyo, Nagoya, Osaka, Kobe—sixty-seven Japanese cities.
> *Fly low, napalm spreads. Smoke rises, clouds our windshields;*
> *no protection against the stench of burning flesh.*

I try to imagine Daddy during the War:
near Okinawa, on Ie Shima,
12-mile oval island ringed by coral:
palm trees, springs of fresh water, sandy beaches
on the south, cliffs on the north, deep cave bunkers.
*It was hot; it rained all the time.*

Three landing strips rebuilt fast, after the U.S. took the island.
Then emergency landing for B-29s, super fortresses;
base for Daddy's 507th Fighter Group's P-47 Thunderbolts:
single engine, cameras and four 50-caliber
machine guns on each wing.

> On Okinawa, ships were massing—
> 42 aircraft carriers, 24 battleships,
> 400 destroyers and destroyer escorts—
> to invade Japan: five times bigger than D-Day.
> Casualty estimates 1-4 million Allies, 5-10 million Japanese.
> We prepared half a million purple heart medals.

Enola Gay landed on Ie Shima after the raid.
Daddy saw the film, did bomb damage assessment.
How many killed by Little Boy and Fat Man?

An Ie Shima Thunderbolt filmed the surrender,
Emperor Hirohito on the USS Missouri.
I have that film. The U.S. hasn't yet used up
those same purple-heart medals. Daddy
came back to paint his roof, to comb gray hair.

*What does it rain?*

## Children. Dolls.

### I. The Antique Baby Doll

My big baby doll smiles, her cheeks glow pink.
Her bright blue eyes, wide open, sparkle in the light.
Her dark brown hair curls up from her face.
She is happy—clean and fresh, in family baby clothes:
embroidered pink cape, flowered dress,
beribboned white booties.

Her name is TaTa. Eiley Tureman named her.
When I was five, Mama Cleary gave TaTa to me.
I dressed TaTa in my sister's baby clothes
and laid her on the fluffy pale fur rug beside my bed.
One day a plumber came to our house. He came upstairs.
He looked into my room. He rushed down the stairs shouting
to Mommy that her baby had fallen to the floor.

> Eiley Tureman was born in 1907. When Eiley grew up, she gave
> TaTa to my grandmother. Now Eiley's big house is a Toy Museum.

### II. The Boy, Omran Daqneesh

His gray clothes and skin and hair
flash drab against the van's orange seat.
Blue bruises flush his face and arms and legs.
His face is blood and dirt over darkening purple.
One eye, red, stares at nothing;
the other, swollen shut.
Hair a thick gray mat, ear a crimson bruise.
A cuddly five-year old, Omran Daqneesh
sits still and dull-faced
in the ambulance in Aleppo, after the bombing.

> Omran Daqneesh was pulled from rubble in Aleppo after an airstrike in an endless war.
> His photograph was on the front page of *The New York Times* on 19 August 2016.

TaTa is too young to walk.
Omran is too tired.
She lies against pale blue cushions.
He sits on the orange ambulance seat.
She is alive.
He was left for dead
under the rubble of Aleppo;
He does not cry or speak.

TaTa reaches up her hands as if to clap;
she is too young to catch a ball.
Omran lifts his hand, wipes his eye,
looks at his dirty hand,
wipes it on the orange plastic seat.


*III. The Soldiers in the Palace Nursery*
When Magi Habsburg was five years old,
Soviet soldiers stomped into her nursery in the palace in Vienna.
She was rocking her big baby doll, singing it to sleep.
Queen Victoria, her grandmother's grandmother, willed her the doll,
big as a toddler, almost too big for Magi to hold.

The soldiers had pistols strapped to their waists, bayonets on their rifles.
One soldier gored the baby doll with his bayonet,
tossed her to another soldier who speared her
and tossed her to another soldier.
The baby doll fell onto the Turkish carpet.
The bayonets tore her flowered dress, eviscerated her,
tossed her into the air again and again.
The soldiers, laughing loudly,
shouting in Russian, stomped out of the room.

Magi never had another doll,
never held another doll,
never wanted another doll.

> Maria Magdalena Habsburg, my classmate at Notre Dame de Sion school in Kansas
> City in the 1950s, told me that in 1947 her mother, Princess Ileana of Romania, had
> asked the soldiers to sit and drink tea in the reception room while she fetched from her
> vault the cash they demanded. First, she secreted her jewels and bank notes to a friend
> who rushed them to Switzerland. Soon after, the family fled to Argentina. Eventually
> they came to the United States.

*IV. Firebombs Over Dresden*
When Niki Dintzner was almost five,
the sirens wailed and her mother shoved her
down the basement stairs to the shelter.
All her family and neighbors huddled and hummed.
Niki was brave but her big baby doll cried and shrieked in terror.
Niki's mother dragged her back up the stairs, ordered her to run to the river.
*Go Go Go.* The doll fell in the garden, the doll caught fire.
The mother screamed *Go Go Go.* The doll vanished. Niki ran to the river.

On 14 February 1945 when the Allies firebombed Dresden, Niki
Dintzner and her mother survived.  Everyone in the shelter perished.

*V. Children.  Dolls*
I want to hold Omran, wash his face, give him supper.
I want to hold Magi when she is five years old,
rock her until she can learn to cry again,
take her and Niki and Omran to get ice cream.

All I can do is smile back at TaTa,
wash and iron her pretty clothes,
wonder about the little girl named Eiley Tureman,
tell the Toy Museum that they can have TaTa.
But not until I die.

> *Can a big baby doll clap her hands?*
> *If fire burns off a toddler's hair, will it grow back?*
> *If a soldier bayonets a baby doll, can the mother sew it up?*
> *Can a child love another doll?*

*Ice Age Bone Circle*

Forty Feet Across, at Kostenki Borshchevo, Near Moscow

When he was a boy, Grandfather said,
the days turned colder, less rain,
the river became smaller,
willow larch aspen clustered on the bank.
His father led the hunters: with their javelins
the men killed many wooly mammoths,
roasted them in charcoal fires.
stored meat deep in the freezing earth,
burned some bones—
*bone burns brighter with less heat—*
piled bones in a huge circle.
Many wooly mammoths killed,
bones bleached, piled up, the circle grew.
All through Father's life,
all through my life, the circle grows,
reindeer and horse bones, teeth—kill butchery.
Skulls, skeletons, tusks.

The days grow ever colder,
a high ash plume floats in from the far south,
sifts over my bone circle.
Yellow acid droplets obscure the sun.
Among the bones I hide my family's treasures—
Grandmother's skull pendants,
Mother's necklace of hollow bird bones,
our rotating drill, sewing needles.
Our small statues of pregnant women
show that life will continue
as the ash slowly buries all our bones.

## The Dog. The Lupins

I. *Now*
Here it is sleeting.
At dusk the real snow starts,
gently at first.
From my bedroom window I watch the snow
which starts to cover the mud and the grass,
the chairs in the courtyard, the bushes, the faded flowers.

From my bedroom window I look over
the garden of my neighbor.
I see his black German shepherd
strolling, ambling, wandering in the garden—
making footprints in the snow,
gray footprints on the virgin snow.

I am alone in my house.
The dog barks. He howls.
The snow is gray.
In the twilight the snow is brown.
In the fog the snow is gray.
The fog. The haze.

I am alone in my brown house.
The neighbor's dog howls in the garden.

I hear the screeching of the train tracks:
crying scandal,
crying for help,
crying for mercy.

The cries of prisoners,
Sobs of ignorance and despair.

The silence of the snow.

Nothing in the courtyard, nothing in the fields.
The forest has disappeared.
The soldiers have sown blue lupins.
Treblinka.

The earth forgets Treblinka.
The snow covers the mud and the grass.
The snow covers even the hypocrite lupins.


*II. Treblinka*
The train stops.
Through the tiny window I see the trees.
I hold my child up to see the green branches.
I smell the pine trees.
The air is fresh and clear.

We will have a shower;
we will have supper;
we will have a bed.

The train tracks screech.

Of what follows, there are no witnesses.
Now nothing in the courtyard.
Nothing in the fields.
No forest. No train tracks.
The soldiers sowed blue lupins.
Blue lupins sway in the breeze,
cover the mud and the pits.
The earth forgets Treblinka.

## A Sharp Wind Blows Through Tall Grasses

Soldier voices from Peter Jackson's WWI film, *They Shall Not Grow Old*

Millions of golden stars in the deep blue heavens.
A sharp wind blows through tall grasses.

Barbed wire so dense a rabbit couldn't get through it.
Going in, you taste the top of your mouth.
We shot them one by one.
Shove your bayonet as hard as you can.
Rifles too hot to fire anymore.
Jets of flame.
Real shooting over in about ten minutes.

Glad to be captured.  Just boys.  Why war?
Hot tea goes down beautifully.  With a dose of rum.

Worst cases were those shot in the chest.
Moaning and groaning, eventual silence.
Die right away, that's best.
If a guy was dead he was no trouble, medically.
Make a barricade of the dead.

3/4 of my men killed or wounded.
1 million British and Empire servicemen killed.

11-11-1918, 11 am:
Silence.
No cheers.
The only way to celebrate
would have been with a mug of tea.
We were exhausted.
We were now redundant.

A sharp wind blows through tall grasses.
Larkspur in the craters,
lilies of the valley in the craters.
Millions of golden stars in the deep blue heavens.

## Zippi Was Tall and Blond

Zippi was tall and blond. She wore a clean jacket
and she smelled good. When I arrived, she spoke
to me, a boy of seventeen. I had
dark curly hair, green eyes. I know I was tall,
and she said I was handsome. Still, very odd there
for a grown woman to speak to a male.

Like everyone else, I was cold and hungry. She gave me
a piece of bread. The next day she gave me her potato.
Every day a little extra food.

Zippi drew up the camp's labor charts. She gave me
a decent schedule. Every day a few people
would fling themselves into the electric fence. My job
was to collect them, drag them to a barracks,
leave them for the guards.

Zippi loved my singing. She had me
entertain the guards at their parties.

Zippi asked me to meet her inside the mountain
of old clothes, a space just big enough for the two
of us.  She did not think seventeen was too young.
She was twenty-five. I knew nothing of what when where.
She taught me everything.  We met every two weeks.
She paid a friend a whole potato to be a lookout.

We planned to meet in Warsaw, in the community center,
when it was all over. But I was rescued
by the Americans, taken to New York.

> We never forgot. Seventy- two years later
> my rabbi son took me to see Zippi in New York.
> She was almost blind, almost deaf.
> We held hands.  I sang for her. We never forgot.

## The Monuments Men

—from *Rescuing DaVinci,* by Robert Edsel

1. *Hitler Loved Art*
*Rome, May 1938* (p.34)
In the Borghese Gallery Hitler stares at
Canova's Pauline Bonaparte.
White marble, life-sized, luminous.
He stares straight at her, his mouth slightly open,
his eyes wide, glistening.

She smiles, but not at him.
She is looking at the frowning Nazi beside him
who stares and grips the steel
railing around her marble couch.
An officer behind Hitler leans
forward just a bit, not quite smiling.

They see soft belly,
 lower limbs draped in white marble,
Roman nose, slender arms, the usual full breasts,
a straightforward gaze.

I do not think any of them loved women.
I do not think they would know how
to touch Pauline Bonaparte LeClerc Borghese
to make her smile from her heart,
let alone to make her suck in her breath or moan.

But she might smile and moan anyway.
She might take on all of those officers
one by one or all at once.  She'd know what to do.

Pauline did not require love.
Hitler, his officers, did not require a virgin.

2. *Fifteenth-Century Eve*
*In Berchtesgaden, June 1945, 101st Airborne Division* (p. 188)
An American soldier stands
face to face with polychrome wooden Eve,

large as life, as tall as himself,
draped to her knees in wavy golden hair,
smiling straight at him,
her head slightly tilted toward him.

His arms hang limp by his sides,
his field glasses protrude at his waist.
He is still, straight, respectful.

They could be meeting for the first time.
They could be falling in love.

3. *Madonna and Child*  (p. 190)
She stands a full head taller
than the two American soldiers
who unload her from a freight car
abandoned at Berchtesgaden.

Her knee bent, she could walk
out of this tomb on her own.
Her polychrome robes
shine in the dim light.

Both soldiers seem to lift her naked infant,
one soldier grasps her waist.
They raise her from her sawdust pedestal,
as she reigns serene.

4. *Ghent Altarpiece*  (p. 199)
Two unidentified soldiers marvel
at the very pregnant life-sized Eve
stuck in her niche and
separated from the Ghent Altarpiece
and from her husband.

One soldier stands several feet away,
stares stoically.

The other stands close,
his hands in his pockets
but leaning forward,
staring at her belly,
as if she were his own wife,
cold and needing a robe.

## No Chiaroscuro

I take Mother to the Mount Baker Wilderness
. . . the slow smokeless burning of decay. Robert Frost, "The Wood-Pile"

Mother hates this Old Growth Forest.
All that death and decay terrifies her.
The standing dead trees, jagged, pointing at nothing,
low trunks chewed off, rasped, snagged.
If under water, a snag could shred a steamboat's hull.

The fallen dead trees, fifty feet, zagging
along the ground, one hundred feet, more.
Odd angles, no pattern, pick-up sticks for Titans.
Fallen trunks jabbing far back into the forest.

Dust hovering, lit up by shafts of sunlight
streaking through the forest's torn canopy.
And everywhere else, dull dark shade,
No shadows, no dappling moving light,
no rustling leaves.

Even the leaves are dim.
All the ashen colors of decaying wood,
the carpet of brown pine needles, of woody debris.
The smell of dust. The sallow odor of
decay. Not the pungent scent of Death.

She can't see that lichens and moss, seedlings
and fungi, insects and small animals flourish
here, that the forest is alive, that it regenerates.
She won't see the thick-trunked thousand-year-old pines.
She doesn't care that woodpeckers and spotted owl
love the standing dead trees—for nesting, for finding grubs.
She is terrified that an owl will swoop at her;
the woodpecker's staccato taps are midnight knocks
on her door, pounding. Silent shouting.

She spies a shadow far back there. A moose?
Bear? Mountain lion? A soldier?
She wants steady predictable light; the sounds
of the city. She wants clippers to form a path,
a broom to sweep up a trail.

I snap her picture beneath an ancient Douglas Fir.
She stares high up, can't see its crown. She trembles.

# III
*Near Death*

### English Bay, Vancouver: Skinny Man Swims Far Out

Low tide.  Little waves.  Slate gray water fades to sky.
Big logs on beach; not fallen, brought there.
My Love and I wind along the shore; hooded windbreaker, drippy umbrella.
Runners, joggers, strollers; canes and toddlers.  Pick-ups on benches.
Above the path, thick forest hides the road.  Slightest turning of colors.
Unseen voices on the beach, laughter behind a rock wall, smell of weed.
Sitting on a log, a couple with a bouncy baby.

An older man, not too old, not too skinny,
pink bathing cap, cord around waist—
yellow buoy twice as big as a basketball, melon-shaped.
Taking a while to adjust cap and cord,
walks down to the cold water, wades up to ankles, knees.
Up to waist.  Waiting at long intervals.
After a long time, starts to swim.  Crawl.  Keeps going.

I think he will swim to the darker water, the shallows, and turn back.
I think he will pass the channel marker, then turn back.
Then the next channel marker, then the next,
Yellow buoy floating out behind him, strong steady strokes, keeps going,
is he heading to the cruise ship?

It keeps going, passes, he veers to the left, farther.
He has disappeared. A gull or a heron, or a goose.
No, I see his strokes, almost too far away to see,
invisible against the dark water.
No sun, all gray sky and water, lights on boats not yet on.

I keep staring, asking people, *Is he going to die?*
The mother of the baby; a Chinese woman:
I ask each one: *Is he going to die?*
*No, I don't think so,* they all reply.
The girl with movie-star bobbed black hair, the slow joggers:
*Is he going to die?  No, I don't think so,* they all reply.

At last, I sit on a bench by two bearded men.
They explain, *They do that.  It's not suicide.*

## The Old Man on the Lawn

The Petrie Court Café of New York's Metropolitan Museum of Art

Too late for brunch, too early for lunch,
famished fasting for a long Mass at Saint Patrick's,
weak from the long bus ride, from loitering too long
in the enormous sumptuous tapestry exhibit,
I mill about, wait for a seat. Then, a window table,
a handsome server—lithe, dark-haired, smiling.

Near the windows, three bronze nudes: Maillol, Rodin:
*L'Ile de France* is fairly svelt, *The Prayer* is large,
*Enchained* is zaftig. A distinguished-looking man
of a certain age, wearing a wedding band,
walks around each nude—slowly, stoically;
he seems not to notice that the bronzes vibrate.

I slowly eat my *frisée* calamari salad,
wish my server were not so busy.
The stiff married man has wandered off.

And through the windows, I see on the lawn an old man
in blue jeans, no shirt, bare-headed, barefoot; his beard
and hair grizzled, hoary; somewhat tanned, skinny
but fairly muscular, like *Socrates* by Jacques-Louis David,
or like an elderly Walt Whitman.

He strolls in full sunlight on the lawn:
he turns, he circles, he twirls around—
sometimes at a quick military pace, then in a funereal march,
he tours the lawn in the bright sunlight.
He has the air of a dancer—I think he is part of a mini-ballet,
of an artistic installation, of a performance piece.

He talks to an invisible interlocutor: he gesticulates—
logically like a professor, deliberatively like a trial lawyer;
then supplicating, imploring, his hands raised in prayer;
now agitated like a windmill.

On the sidewalk which encloses the old man's lawn,
crowds pass by—the young on bicycles, lovers arm in arm,
old people on canes, babies in strollers, businessmen with briefcases—

no one pays attention to the old man—to all he is invisible.

But an old woman with stylish hair, in a camel-hair suit,
alligator pumps and purse, stands still on the sidewalk,
her eyes wide open, and stares at the old man on the lawn.
He does not notice her.

Precisely at noon he disappears from my sight;
I become worried, get up to look for him.
But suddenly he reappears with a sack that says
*I Heart New York*. He circles the lawn twice

and stops in the middle.  From his sack
he takes out an orange.  He contemplates
his orange, he speaks to it. He peels his orange, slowly.
He sits down on the lawn, and, while rocking
his orange, he eats it, with tiny little bites.

My server offers me dessert. He explains that
          since the beginning of spring
          the old man has spent all of each day
          on the lawn.  One lovely afternoon
          in May a passerby offered him
          an iced tea and a sandwich.

          The sandwich the old man tore up right there,
          and the tea he let pour out onto the grass.
          The Samaritan left, his head bowed down.

          The Museum published an article
          about the old man on the lawn;
          his family in the South read the article
          and came to New York to find him,
          but the old man hit at his relatives
          and they left, their heads bowed down.

          Since then, no one pays him any attention.
          But they worry about him as winter approaches.

I order the chocolate bomb cake, stare at the bronzes.
Wish someone would compare me to *L'Ile de France*?
The café is now noisy and my server has disappeared.

## It Was Always the Jewels

*Sergis Bauer in Gaslight: Paula, it was always the jewels between us.*

I.
The jewels, where are they, where could they be?
They must be hidden here in her attic. I moved
all of her things up here when I married her niece,
Paula, that stupid girl, she thinks I love her.

It is only the jewels. Surely they are in a drawer,
perhaps wrapped in a silk scarf, perhaps
in an ornate box, a coffer heavily carved,
or in a small brocade casket; surely
they are here. Perhaps they fell loosely onto
the floor, scattered behind an armoire, perhaps
under the cushion in this upholstered chair,
perhaps inside the upholstery. I slash it with
her kitchen knife, I slash her silk undergarments
so neatly folded, every pale color, jewel-colored lingerie.

Where are those diamonds, the huge yellow diamonds?
Light streaming like the sun, all fire day and night,
luscious blinding fire, enormous yellow diamonds
glowing like hot coals, flaming out
from her fingers and wrists, from her diadem,
every time she sang from the stage, glowing in the limelight.

I can feel them, they burn my hands, where are they?
I slash and slash, I rip apart her armoires, her books.
She was such a stupid woman, surely she would hide them
in her books, her upholstery, her lingerie,
surely I can find them, should find them after searching,
slashing night after night, for weeks and weeks.

II.
Paula thinks I am critical. No, I just
want to drive her mad, then I can
commit her; then I can have her house to search
all day every day in the daytime.

Yes, in the light of day I could see clearly,
would not need the fickle gaslight. Paula

thinks she imagines the flickering. Let her keep
thinking, soon she will believe she is mad.

When I send her away, I can burn the house down:
the jewels will not melt in the fire, they will shine out,
they will flame out. I will find them.
Alice Alquist's jewels will at last be mine,
Alice Alquist's jewels will be mine.

## The Bridge

He walked toward me rolling a cigarette,
and when he got close I saw
that the cigarette was fat,
with a bulge in the middle,
and strands golden in the sunlight
were hanging out at each end.

His eyes were blue like the river,
and frost was collecting
on the hairs of his nose.

  *—Ma'am, you shouldn't be sitting there.*
  *—It's okay. I do this all the time.*

The sky and water were the same color
and the cool air swirled around my ankles.
I took off my shoes and just let my feet dangle.

A fish was swimming kind of funny
just below me.
It thrashed and floated,
like it was fighting
but wasn't very strong.

The man finished rolling his cigarette,
and I expected him to light it fancy,
like in the old movies—
strike a wooden match on his boot
or his hip or his fingernail –
but he just held it cupped
in his left hand
out of the wind,
and the other hand
reached out into the air
toward me.

  *—Ma'am, it's not really safe out there.*
  *—Don't worry, I just want to feel the breeze.*

The sky was streaking red and gray.

*—Ma'am, this is private property.*
*You really shouldn't be here*
*—So, can you stop someone*
*from watching the sunset?*

I put my elbows on my knees
and watched all the colors
concentrate into one orange ball.

*—Ma'am, please.*
*Take my handkerchief.*

He reached a red bandana toward me.
He came out onto the girders,
not tentative like a tightrope walker,
but firm-footed,
like he was walking on his own front porch.
He looked a little older than I,
but with a lot of creases between his eyes
that didn't belong there.

*—I like it here.*
*—Is that your car, Ma'am?*
*Let me walk you back to your car.*

The colors stopped moving. I stood up.
I took his hand, and stepped over
to the middle of the bridge.
Through the rails the water looked dark.
I dabbed at my eyes with the bandanna.

*—I work here, Ma'am.*
*Do you want to tell me about it?*

We were on the gravel now,
and he lit his cigarette,
a match from the Smokestack Bar-B-Que.
The paper flared up
and little tendrils of tobacco glowed
and then flaked white.

Before they reached the ground
they got too small to see.

     *—Ma'am. Please. Here, sit down.*

He sat me down on a big rock
and stood beside me.
His bronze belt buckle
was a sculpture of this very bridge—
The first railroad bridge over the Missouri.

     *—Ma'am, let me wipe your face.*
     *Would you care for a drag off my cigarette?*

     *What the hell,* I thought.

     *—Sure. Thanks.*

It scratched my throat and I coughed.
His arms were around my shoulders
and I was staring into his shirt.
It smelled like dry leaves and sunlight.

     *—Ma'am, I take it you're married.*
     *Don't you need to be with your husband now?*

Two men were swaggering up the path.
They wore guns and Texas hats.

     *—Ma'am, they're the bridge police.*
     *I'll talk to them.*

He went down the path.
The guards were shouting and gesticulating,
but I couldn't hear the voice
of the man with the cigarette.

The downtown lights were coming on
and the sunset was darkening,
but the sun was still a fiery ball.
I sat on my hands.
Underneath me I felt a loose stone.

I curled my fingers around it.
It felt like a statue.

The three men came back up the hill.

> —*Look, Girlie, we won't press charges*
> *if you leave right now. Quiet-like.*

I pulled the stone out
from under me
and examined it.
It was shaped
like a little person.

> *Litho,* stone.
> *Pediens,* child.

That was what I had.
Sepsis, if it didn't come out;
lacerations if it tried to come out.
And if doctors tried to get it out?
My stone, my statue, my child.

I stood up,
The stone light against my fingers.
I couldn't toss it into the river.
I didn't want to leave it on the ground.

The man with the cigarette
took my other hand
and led me to my car.

*My Sister Died on Christmas*

I.
Like Grandfather,
Sister died on Christmas.
I decorate her coffin
with bare branches
of their talking tree.

Mother Superior
and the infirmarian,
white-veiled
link arms behind me
as I sing

II.
We rubbed her back in
sweet-scented liquid.
She stopped writhing.
I felt dizzy.
She stopped moaning.

III.
We never killed
What they said we killed.
We never ate
what they said we ate.
There was no cat.

## Mount Everest Cries Out

Sagarmatha, Peak of Heaven, Goddess Mother of the World,
you want to be worshipped from afar.
The full moon hides behind you,
airplanes fly close,
but your worshippers want to embrace you,
to caress you on all sides.

You wrap yourself in ice and snow and howling winds.
You send your Khumbu Glacier sliding down;
your river of ice advances five feet every normal day,
and sometimes it rushes, avalanches.
Not even your Sherpas can keep up
with the Glacier's shifting crevasses,
its snow bridges fluffing over the void,
its suddenly collapsing ice towers.

Crystal walls ten stories high shine
in all the colors of the moon,
glacier snow glows turquoise blue,
black crevasses crack down to the center of the earth,
enclosing the bodies of those who dare to caress you.

And still your worshippers trek up your sides:
aluminum ladders, crampons, ice axes, spike into your face.
Oxygen bottles, bright frayed tents, litter your lap;
refuse from your worshippers' digestive tracts
flows down your sides.

Your worshippers gasp, they vomit, they collapse. They die.
Still, they keep climbing.
Your howling winds do not stop them,
Oh Goddess Mother of the World.

## Oh Congo, My Love

The illiterate Congo children will burden the country for the half-century ahead.
—Nicholas D. Kristof, *International Herald Tribune*, 21 May 1997

If those children were mine, I would
teach them to read.  I would open
up their heads, with a little knife
I'd slit their foreheads right across
and stuff in words like garlic cloves,
and the perfume of those words would
seep and spread like lilies in a
hotel lobby, like roses from
a bridal bouquet right out of
their brains and form in the air like
umbrellas and parasols and
little clouds, would rise from their huts
like water vapor from lakes on
distant hills after spring rains; and
the words would pull those children's limbs
up like arms that feel light after
plaster casts have been sawn off, and
those children would dance around the
house, and help me sweep the dirt yard
and edge the path with glass shards from
bottles blue and green and brown, and
we'd bake mud bricks in the sun and
build another bedroom and another.

But then, I don't know, because
Lumumba and Mobutu and
now Kabila—is one worse than
another, and what of the King
Leopold and our diamond
and copper and gold mines?
What of our coffee and rubber and banana
plantations?  The jungle has seized
our diamond and copper and
gold mines, our coffee and rubber
and banana plantations.  The
jungle has seized Stanleyville's dance
pavilions and concert halls, our
majestic aedifices and
stately boulevards, our gilded palm-lined

capital.  The ageing children
of our poets sell charcoal on
the streets, on the curbside they hawk
cakes and palm oil, salt soap sugar
lemonade.  The young mother sells
her beauty at the Take-a-Peek
Café.  Her grandfather owned a
bicycle, a sewing machine,
a battery radio, a
hand-crank phonograph.  Her sister
took a first at University;
now she presides unpaid over
the library's broken windows, lonely
books.  All our schools closed long ago.

Still, if those children were mine, I'd
force words into their skulls, I'd make
them sweep the yard.  And with machetes
we would subdue the jungle, we'd
cultivate orchids in faience
urns along our Great Brown Congo.

## As the Firefly Passes through Flame

after Saint Francis de Sales, *Introduction to the Devout Life, 1609*
sonnet for the inauguration of a university president
*To study is a good way to learn; to hear is a still better way;*
*but to teach is the best of all.* —Erasmus
*The office of teaching serves as a foundation for learning.* —St. Augustine


As the firefly passes through the flames and does
not singe its wings; as the pearl oyster flourishes
in the fresh spring in the midst of the salt sea,
so you, oh Philothea, my child in love with God,
may live Devoutly in towns, in families, at court,
in the mechanic's shop, and on the battlefield.

The florist arranges bouquets in vast variety;
with His many voices, the Spirit inspires His children,
loves His wild array of blooms—His mechanics
and teachers and soldiers.

              Every colored jewel
shines brighter when coated in honey, as your life, Philothea,
gains luster through Devotion.

              In study, hearing,
teaching, you may shine through honey, fly
through flames, find fresh water in the sea.

## Arise, O Daughter of Sion

for Lenore's Birthday and Funeral

*Arise arise, put on thy strength, O Sion,*
*put on the garments of thy glory. Loose*
*the bonds from off thy neck, O captive daughter.*
*How beautiful upon the mountains are*
*the feet of him that bringeth good tidings, and*
*that preacheth peace. Rejoice and give praise together,*
*O ye deserts of Jerusalem.* (Isaias 52, 1-9)

On the eve of All Saints Day, as the rain paused, late
in the raw afternoon, I stepped out into my garden.
A wisp of smoke, a small cloud, a mist,
hung in the air near my rose bush. As I noticed
it, it took a shape, floated—not as if blown,
but moving of its own accord—from east to west,
across the brick path, quickly, but not
precipitously; deliberately, not random; planned—
in a straight line in front of me;
and dissolved, disappeared, was no longer
visible, but was not necessarily gone;
just long enough for me to see it clearly,
to be aware, to be sure.

*Requiem aeternam dona ea Domine,*
*et lux perpetua luceat ea.*
*Eternal rest grant unto her, O Lord,*
*and let perpetual light shine upon her.*
*A hymn becomes you, O God, in Sion,*
*Listen to my prayer, unto you all flesh shall come,*
Duruflé sings his Requiem

When last I saw her, she said she would come
to see me on her way out, would keep
in touch. Can she see me now?
On my dresser I array her gifts:
Wharton and Brodsky books, French perfume,
a Japanese lacquer box, a Russian spoon.
I wear her silk blouse, mohair coat,
bias skirt, sleek black shoes. So arrayed,
could I take on her wisdom with this beauty?

At my last visit, she was too sick to see me,
so Alison showed me her mother's garden.
Along precise small paths, we wandered luxurious
color and scent. Delicate yellow abutilon,
green zinnias, Mexican sunflower, tuberoses,
white delphinia, Graham Thomas roses,
dogwood. Herbs—rosemary, basil, curry,
thyme, mint, lemon verbena. Variegated Hosta;
coxcomb, sedum, spider wort, purple wisteria;
Russian sage against the wall. Kansas prairie grass.
And her prize, her moon vine. It blooms every afternoon
at four—huge, luminous white blossoms.
It closes just before sunrise.  We saw the buds.

## Budapest Street Scene

Two sisters in father's new car

Those girls were alive.
>    *Yes, we'll get your Porsche home by midnight.*
>    *We're going to the Portside Bar.  All our friends go there.*
>    *We love the Cuban music.*
They met university students from Munich.
They drank Golden Pheasant Slovak beer.
They sang, they danced, they planned a picnic at the zoo tomorrow.
All those cute boys, the summer breeze,
The girls' darling little skirts and spike-heeled sandals.
Those girls were alive.

One boy said,
>    *Last spring a girl disappeared from the Portside Bar.*
>    *After a while, the police stopped looking.*
>    *The parents came in from Rumania.*
>    *Heavy equipment dredges the Danube.*
>    *They found her two kilometers downriver from the Chain Bridge.*

It was late, but not that late.
But they hurried home along Vaci Street,
heading for the Elizabeth Bridge, to Kossuth Lajos Street.
It was late but not too late.

The utility pole came out of nowhere.
The flames came out of nowhere.
The paramedics tried to open the doors.
The flames came out of nowhere.
The paramedics tried.
It was late but not that late.
Those girls were alive.

## Budapest Midnight

The last two years the old couple next door has been dying.
Mr. Vodas wore pajamas over his clothes,
thought his shirt was trousers; Mrs. Vodas had strokes.
The thin frail son came every month, then every week, every day.

Last midnight, I woke to pounding on my door.
Don't answer—some of the neighbors are crazy.
Out the window, I see a police car.
Pounding, shouting. *Who is it?*

Blood splatters in the corridor,
bloody footprints, blood in the elevator.
An old woman shouting, screaming in the hallway.
She saw a pool of blood downstairs in the entry,
bloody footprints leading to the elevator.
No sounds of a fight, but so much blood.

We all pounded on the door next to my apartment.
We pounded and called out. We heard moaning.

The door was unlocked.
My young neighbor lay slumped in an armchair,
a bloody towel to his face, moaning, mumbling, incoherent.

Ambulance.
Gurney could not fit into the elevator.
Carry him down five flights.

The story: His mother died this day last month.
Father died this day last year.
Long illnesses, strokes, dementia.
Inherited apartment, still untidy.
The son, so serious, so thin, went out drinking.
Slipped in the entryway, hit his head
against the trash bin, gashed his temple.

## Mother, the Imelda Marcos of Mink

*(The First Lady of the Philippines owned an estimated 3000 pairs of shoes.)*

Mother doesn't have that many shoes,
and most are black flats because of her poor tired feet.
First it was ordinary bunions, corns, calluses.
Then the bloated macerated toe.
She knew about macerating dried apricots in brandy for a pie,
*but what is a macerated toe?* she asked the orthopedic nurse.
On the nurse's orders, every morning, Mother soaked that toe
in hot soapy water, swabbed it with betadine, taped a cotton ball to it.
After six months that toe dried up and the puffy skin fell off,
and left a bright red crater. But the pain stopped.

Still, Mother could not wear pretty shoes.
She gave her four-inch purple velvet stiletto pumps
to her six-foot-tall sixteen-year-old granddaughter,
who wore them with a red leather miniskirt to
Thanksgiving lunch at the Country Club.
Now Mother's shoes are black flats, as fancy as she can find:
calfskin, crocodile, patent leather, silk;
gold edged, silver-buckled, sequined.
Nevertheless, she feels old and short.

Thus her new quest, the furs. All mink, except for
—the ancient forbidden, hidden, Somali leopard;
—the vintage blue fox shoulder wrap,
for which she awaits a debutante ball or a winter wedding;
—and the new huge tailored not-your-grandfather's racoon
which she would wear to a frigid football game were she invited.

Her partial mink inventory, from years of searching:
—her mother's 1950s stole, repurposed into a suede and fur bomber jacket;
—the worn-out Black Glama now lining a Khrushchev-style fullback-
        shaped purple raincoat;
—the floor-dragging one-size-fits-all swirl-patterned Empress-of-Russia cape;
—the boxy vintage Joan Crawford white shorty;
—the knee-length reversible brown all-weather, her only appropriate daywear coat;
—and just now, finally, the classic fits-right long-haired ankle-length ranch,
the one she would have should have bought first had she found it.
Now—at last—her furrier has retired, so she has to stop buying.
All her furs are natural colors—no iridescence: no ruby-red or hot pink or lavender.
All classic cuts—no trailing snaky boas or Brunhilde vests; no trousers or miniskirts.

She does not want to look young or trendy or odd;
she aims for glamour, elegance. She hopes to feel gorgeous.

All this luxury energizes her away from a nursing home, propels her
to endless errands to post office and gas station and grocery store.
Her social life is gala receptions after cathedral funerals.

All her friends wear cloth or puffer coats.
She channels Margot Channing, Elizabeth Taylor, Maria Callas.
She has large glass emeralds and diamonds—matching necklace and earrings.
She yearns for the balls and banquets of yesteryear.
And every evening she festoons herself in the fur of the moment,
pats it like a puppy, strokes its long silky pelt. Dreams.

## Drink

*I don't care what the people are thinkin', I ain't drunk, I'm just drinkin'.* —Albert Collins
*You can lead a horticulture but you can't make her think.* —Dorothy Parker
*Say anything you like about me, except that I drink water.* —W. C. Fields

I.
In front of All-Star Automotive in the college town,
a burned-out car: silver-black, dusty gold;
melted tires, charred seats. Car a black skeleton.

And the bodies?
Did they all escape? Or just some? How many?
Ambulance? Hospital?

Country road?
Impact—tree, wall, building?
Another car?
Person?

How much drinking?

II.
My friends don't drink as much as they used to.
How long does beer last in a refrigerator?
Will it go bad in a year? In two?
What makes beer bad?
My brother had malaria. Two friends are in AA.
Are we old? *Many are cold but few are frozen.*
I need to buy more Sprite.

III.
Where have all the flowers gone?
My parties end now by eight o'clock.
No one stays to watch the sunset.
No one stays to light the candles.

I had the brass candelabra lacquered,
bought hurricane globes to spread, refract the light.
I scrubbed ceramic sconces, dozens of votives.

All one summer I made love with a young man
in the far corner of the garden,
our only light from an antique ship's lantern
high on the porch's white pillar.

## Cadaver Bone, Donor-Cycle

At the dentist's, an old lady regrets.

I wish I had not done it.  Could it have been avoided?
Why is this happening? I wish I had waited—
then I could have died from something else.

I smell bone: fresh ground-up bone,
burning bone. Bone fragments spray my face.

I taste the drugs, they paralyze my tongue.
I taste my blood. I still feel the needle.

*Close your eyes, don't look at the needle.*
Water splashing, spraying. Light on, off.
Odd sounds—whirrs, grinding, clicks.
The smells of bone, of blood, of fire.
Pressure; bone water blood spraying.
*Close your eyes.*
My feet are cold. I have to pee. Can I still walk?

Sewing the bone graft, cadaver paté, was it from a nice person?
Sewing the collagen seal, I feel the stitches, the pricks over and over.

      Motorcycle flies over the guard rail,
      soars far down into the canyon; donor-cycle.

            I'm paying for my youthful folly—
            sneaking out during Mother's nap
            to kiss the little boys across the street,
            flying down the bumpy sidewalk,
            soaring over my tricycle handlebars—
            bloody mouth, smashed baby teeth, smashed bone.

I see two Aztec pointy teeth, two bloody sockets.
I'm  dizzy. Swollen. Sore. Too sore for kissing.

Why don't they have pretty pictures on the ceiling?
Fluffy bunnies, lilacs, children playing.

      It was necessary.
      Was it truly necessary?
      I wish I had not done it.

## Wrong Road: Driving in Kansas

Low gray sky, gravel road, sharp winding.
No trees, dead trees.  No shadows.
Where there is no light there are no shadows.

And where the sun shines hard on the prairie
there are no shadows:
with a tree there is a shadow;
under a bridge there is a shadow;
mottled clouds cast shadows.

When the sun lights up the winter prairie
the bleak day turns gold;
when the sun shines it is colder—
the clouds hold in some warmth.

If we were in the woods
all would be gray
if all the sky were gray.

Ice, mud, tundra.
No color.
No light.
Cold.
*Deer Crossing.*
No deer.

At home, boots caked with frozen mud.
Slow fat raccoon right by the back door,
sniffing bread crusts.
Did you see the possum in the shadows?
What makes the shadows?
I do not hear the coyote howl.
Keep the raccoon off the roof.

You are beside me—
why am I cold,
why afraid?

Persephone is gone.
Persephone eats pomegranate seeds.
far below.

## Ashes Ruffle in the Breeze

A cool day in spring, no sun, no wind.
I pile up a basket of old dossiers,
fill the Weber grill to overflowing.
Sensitive papers: letters of recommendation, bank statements;
bad memories: report cards, family counsellor report,
bad personnel review, letter of termination,
*this candidate is less than mediocre*;
broken engagement, guest lists for the cancelled reception,
depositions, divorce decree.

A fire needs fuel, oxygen, accelerant.
It can die if not tended. Oxygen cannot
penetrate a thick dossier's close pages.
Who would have thought
the dossiers would take so long to burn?

Prodding, lifting the pages; gray smoke,
then tiny flames, leaping flames.
Fireplace poker's wooden shaft catches fire.

A sudden breeze, suddenly wind,
too much wind, shifting,
thick smoke wraps around me, envelopes me,
swaddles me in swirling smoke.

A rhapsody in gray and black, not just an arrangement,
more dynamic than Whistler, never static:
pages fan out, curl and undulate, ruffle and fluff.
Black intensifies to all gradations of gray,
to pewter, silver, pearl, at last to white,
the world before Oz, before technicolor,
all the photos of bombed-out cities.

Ash flying everywhere. Why I don't want to be cremated.
An incinerator full of ruffles. Ashes disintegrating, sifting,
wafting, blowing. Bad memories gone.

Kettle still smolders. Dust, powder, blow across
the new green grass. I sift the powder around
the azaleas, full-blooming fuchsia. Fat bunnies cavort.
Robins, cardinals hop, swoop. A woodpecker drills staccato.

*Laocoön's Scream*

I.      Plaster Casts
One hot summer day I wandered into
the Cast Room—slightly cooled but stuffy, dusty—
of Oxford's Ashmolean Museum. Dozens of molded
plaster copies of Greek and Roman sculptures
for students to envision those ancient works.
Before me, Laocoön writhing. Why was I
not moved? Why was I distressed?

II.     Laocoön
The twin pythons coil and uncoil
on Tenedos's calm sea,
rear their blood-red crests,
thrash the wine-dark foam;
undulate across, beslime, the Trojan plain.
As Laocoön, Poseidon's priest by lot
that day, his two young sons beside him,
raises his knife against the massive bull,
Troy's offering to the watery god,
the pythons gliding swiftly
catch the priest's upraised hand,
enwrap his loins, his legs and arms,
coil and twist around his sons,
lunge their fangs at Laocoön's neck.
The smaller child faints from the poison,
the older boy struggles to escape.
Drenched in gore, his head-bands black with venom,
the priest wails in furious agony.

Laocoön angered Poseidon—for what?
Marrying, though a celibate priest?
Caressing his wife in the sacred temple?
Spearing the Trojan horse?
Punished for being right or being wrong.
Agony with no redemption, no reward.

III.    The Sculpture
Virgil and the sculptors record the struggle.
First the words. Then the statue—
how did it begin? Clay mold, wax mold?
Bronze? Marble? Which came first—

Greek? Roman copy? Who gave it life?

In the Roman vineyard of Felice de Fredis,
Michelangelo and Sangallo, *père et fils*,
watch the pope's workmen wrench Laocoön,
fifteen centuries lost, from his muddy grave.
They scrub and polish, resculpt, restore
the lost right arm, send the twisting group
to Pope Julius II.

In the Vatican Museum, marble Laocoön
emits reflects light, pulses with life.
He breathes, convulses, shrieks in agony
as the pythons enwrap his legs, attack his jugular.

Oxford's plaster Laocoön does not shriek.
Smooth white, opaque, matte, dull,
flat, no shine, no light, no breath, no sound, no life.
Why is this Laocoön so dead?
Molds are not wrong. The Ancients used them always:
lost wax, clay, copies in bronze and marble.
Is the Vatican Laocoön a copy of a copy too?
Why do I hate the Ashmolean cast?
Why does the ancient Roman marble writhe and scream
while the plaster mold makes no sound, emits no light?

# Lilies

*We blossom and flourish, like leaves on the tree,*
*Then wither and perish, but nought changeth thee.* —St. Denio

Easter lilies, rubrum lilies trumpet her perfection,
thornless roses drape her body, protecting my Madonna.
Rose satin hides the wooden bier, doves coo in silver cages;
she watches bluebirds soaring free across the painted ceiling.

We've brushed the green silk draperies, polished the walnut paneling with beeswax.
In the parlour where I keep vigil night after night, I will her flowers
to stay fresh forever, I will her to live. She will stay here with me, and each day
I will add more lilies and roses. While they perfume the air, she abides with me.

But the flowers flow backward to their source, they sphacelate.
Before they liquefy, I will dip each one in white wax,
layer after layer, fresh forever; still perfumed, she lives.

Lovely and lively, all covered with lilies,
I keep my Madonna, she flies from her cage—
We soar to the heavens with bluebirds and doves.

## Warmer Than Yesterday

A sunny day, no clouds, warmer than yesterday.
Driving along a side road, a through road,
far on the east side, toward downtown.
No traffic, no traffic lights.

*Turn left here*, says my passenger.
I don't turn. I keep on going.
Empty houses, stone steps up to empty lots.
Old twigs and tree stumps, brown dust.

A sunny day, no clouds, warmer than yesterday.
I keep on going, block after block.

Turn left into a green yard,
lush with spiking spirea, forsythia, miniature willows.
All helter skelter swirling an old yellow metal chair,
not rusted, just old. A red gnome, a blue Virgin Mary.
Up the five porch steps, painted not recently but not too long ago.

A nurse is just leaving,
*I was just going to put him to bed.*
*He is sleeping peacefully.*

The room is all diagonals.
The TV on a metal stand with its back to us.
I walk around the TV and a chair, under a Boston fern.

He is lying on a flat-out pallet, maybe a low gurney.
He is gaunt like a prophet on a cathedral arch,
tan, shiny face, sort of cigar-colored.
I see just his face.  He is swathed in a blanket,
his eyes are closed, he seems asleep, not dead.
The shift nurse leaves, the new one saunters in,
starts to pull the gurney into the middle of the tiny crowded room,
*Let's go back in your room for your nap.*
Pink-sweatered rosy-cheeked nurses.

Who is this man—
sculpted by Donatello?
So thin, like old wood, smooth-faced.

Where am I?  Why am I here?
I do not know.
I am calm.

## Mother Is Dying

for Sarah Curran

Her doctor says my mother is dying.
Mother is, my mother is dying,
dying.  He says, *Your mother is dying.*

She is beautifully groomed and bejewelled.
She has not told us.  Every day she dresses
and puts on her makeup and sits in her chair.

She has not told us—my mother is dying.
Mother is    Mother    is   cancer floating
beautifully groomed dying beautifully

in blue gown, blue mother-of-the-bride
blue satin, blue lace—floating in blue
negligée, sitting swathed in warmed

satin quilts, Mother is talking,
not telling, not letting—her hands resting,
long white fingers, blue jewels, blue veins

so white hands, picking her blue quilt's
silk binding, talking, not letting—
chasing me down in her car.  I race

through pine trees, she's stalking me down
through some field to the edge of some
winter-covered swimming pool, I slip

under the icy blue cover, trip—
down steep concrete stairs into my
blue world, swirling blue, speeding speeding

bullet dolphin speeding to crash
of shouts clapping gold trophy trophies
shouts clapping and my mother has
                    *cancer cancer cancer is dying.*

# IV
*Near Love*

## At That Moment

At that very moment, my fingers were claws of light,
lasers, long, cutting the air, floating
on the ends of my hands, white light, yellow
blue white.  Pointing, they lit, not scraped,
not cut, illuminated your face, slid over,
smoothed your face, fluffed and curled your hair.
White light up to stars, the stars shooting
whirling, spinning, sifting floating down.

And in the crook of your neck, the hollow of your shoulder,
where my face rests, where I kiss your hard strong flesh,
inhale your scent, I pull back my face, jerk up
my neck; and in the hollow dark, light streaking
its shadows, a small friendly bat face, like a plush
rabbit's; like my bat ring: the Chinese man said,
*That bat is blind.* This bat is soft and kindly,
dark in the hollow of your neck, and I pull my face
back out of the hollow, and the bat face is light all white
and golden.  And I scream and you hold me, clutch me hard.
*Yes. Oh, Baby,* and *Yes,* we laugh, *yes YES.*

*Snow Blossoms*

White blossoms waft through April air
like snow fluff,
drift onto new grass,
dot fresh asphalt.

Each spring my Bradford pear tree
bursts into snowy flowers, showers
white petals, blankets the grass.
Every fall it flames out gold
vermilion, lights the sky.

Last year before the red leaves dropped,
early blizzard howled, lightning attacked:
snow and ice and more snow swirled and roiled;
snow and ice and more snow surged
onto leafy branches, reeled them to the ground.
The trunk cracked, split; cascaded into the street.
Neighbors cut it up, hauled off the debris.
But half the tree snapped back up—tall.

Yesterday my half-tree bloomed,
exploded fluffy white.

Today at dawn a chainsaw grinds,
my blooming pear tree shudders, bends.  Collapses.
Flowering branches strewn, heaped high,
like layers of discarded lace petticoats.

Two city trucks: *tree cannot be saved.*

> *Long ago in Portugal, Princess Gilda yearned*
> *for the snow of her Far North homeland*
> *that blanketed and silenced all the earth.*
> *To comfort her, her prince, Ibn Almuncim,*
> *planted thousands of flowering almond trees.*
> *Princess Gilda stopped weeping*
> *when she saw those trees blooming*
> *as far away as the sea.*

White blossoms waft through April air
fluff like snow, drift onto new grass.

## Perhaps a Ruined Abbey

When I think of you, I see an archway—
mossy, cool, of scratchy granite, ancient
Roman gateway to—I cannot tell:
perhaps a ruined abbey, Norman cloister
where monks still chant; or Gothic Salisbury
Cathedral, bombed-out and half-restored.  Some
might build a party palace, restaurants, condos.
I do not know: this field that stretches far
away and even to the wine-dark sea;
a low green plain, a wasteland where something
used to be—or never was or will be;
a wilderness; a field where sheep could safely
graze, where a child could wander; an edge,
a precipice down which a child could abruptly
tumble, grab a protruding root, hang shrieking
unheard above the black and roiling rocks.

I do not know; I cannot see beyond
the arch; I do not see the building or even
the wall from which the arch springs.  I do
not know if it is a monastery.   There are
green vines, but no clematis or wisteria.
Somehow I know it is Spring.  The air is moist;
no rain, neither hot nor cold.  The path is sandy,
damp.  The grass on either side is closely cropped.
It's a low Roman arch, just wide enough for two
to pass abreast.  Perhaps it leads to Italy;
but this seems more like England.  I can't tell
if you are on the path behind or beside
or in front of me.  I can't tell if you are here
at all.  I feel your presence, but I don't
know where you are.  I approach the gate, close
my eyes, lean against the stone, feel
its cool smooth surface against my cheek.

## The First Mermaid: Atargatis, Life of the Waters

I.
That shepherd boy had green eyes
and flaxen hair that swirled across his shoulders.
On the rocky hillside we wove flowers into each others' hair,
and laughed at the sheep who frolicked into and out of the woods.
We rescued the lambs from the brambles,
ringed our fingers with their tangled wool.

Partway down the hillside, in a shallow cave
we rested from the afternoon sun.
On the rough walls we drew our own symbol:
interlocking ellipses, long and slender;
we gave it an eye and a fluttery tail, called it *ichthys*.

As the flowers faded and the leaves began to fall,
my belly swelled, but my golden shepherd boy
had moved on to another hillside far away.
Perhaps he died.
Perhaps I killed him.

At the foot of our hillside
I threw myself into the Pool of Shame.

But I did not drown.
I fluttered my legs and they became a tail.
The fish in the pool rocked me to the shore.
 I bore an egg and the doves hatched it into my lovely daughter.
 I named her *Semiramis*.
We asked Zeus to thank the fish
by giving them stars in the heavens,
and we called that constellation *Pisces*.

II.
Now my shame is forgotten.
My home is a temple with a golden ceiling and a golden door,
and I am all gold, clothed in jewels from many lands,
enthroned on two lions, holding a fish-spear and a distaff.
The ruby in my crown lights up my temple.
Sitting beside me on two bulls is my consort Hadad.
We rule the cities, I fertilize the fields and the waters.

Near my temple is my sacred lake
where the fish are bejeweled pets
and my priests cavort with them,
 and only the priests may eat them.
In front of my temple my priests
chant and dance to drums and flutes,
they bend their necks so low and they whirl so fast
that their hair flies out, it undulates in fiery waves.

The priests built columns like phalluses,
they climb up in the spring.
I think their dancing is too wild,
I deplore and forbid their self-mutilation.
Castration does not help fertility.

III.
When I walk the fields I wear a long tight dress
embroidered with grains of barley;
wheat sheaves on my shoulders; flowers in my hands.
My golden hair waves like the sea.

I am Astarte and Aphrodite and Atargatis,
all the love goddesses of Syria.
I bring life to the waters.
I bring life to the fields.
My doves bring love to all who worship me.

## Golden Morning

Anniversary

White kitchen dawn-striped, cold gold bottle,
best French, I rub wet beaded against my satin
nightgown—I'm still a cantilevered miracle—
thigh-grip pull, pop shot Moët & Chandon
on silk flesh, bubbles on rose-polished toes.

I dip a strawberry in champagne—fat,
fresh, red shadowed—red as my moons'
ebb and flow / post partum, post post post
how long since / how long, I long long
suck red pulp, swirl hot juice around

under tongue, chin dripping, juice, suck
pulp, bite off green, scratchy leaves.
If I dip one for you, where are you:
still in bed, exercising, shower—
will you smile, will you see me

will you forget your Blonde Bond Trader?
Please don't make me invite her to our party.
Aren't I still your dancer, greyhound, racehorse?
Would you suck the strawberry from my fingers?

## Will You Brush my Hair?

*Dahlin', It Don't Mean a Thing.* —Col. JoZach Miller III

This new one, I can't teach him—
His back hurts; he needs a drink, a nap;
to watch the ballgame, read the paper, pay bills.
I can't teach him.

But I remember—
        Hold my face in your hands,
        brush my hair until it grows out
        long and blond in the moonlight.
        Stand with me in the summer rain
        in the midnight garden
        beside the Venus fountain;
        lie with me on the lawn,
        watch the stars.

This new one will not brush my hair.

But: he will not disappear with the morning dew.

Had he been here all along
I would not have needed
someone to brush my hair.

## Peacock Hands

*The Manicurist Speaks*
Her hands are claws, old peacocks',
like Mama's grandma's, picking lint
from her embroidered sheets,
she shrieks for her daughter,
all her children are dead.
This lady smiles when I rub
her wrists, massage her fingers,
pull them like teats.
I need a smoke.

*The Customer Speaks*
Her hands are soft, warm, big
as a man's.  She needs a boyfriend,
her eyelashes are tarantulas,
she needs to pluck that chin hair,
I hope she goes dancing tonight.
Stefan doesn't see my puffed veins,
his hands are brown-spotted, thick.
He dreams of my long red nails
on his chest, dreams of my hands.

## At Sabbatini's

My new purse, the dearest in Florence,
is black butter.  No gold doodads.
We glide to the best table.
Our glistening window reveals
a tiny courtyard garden
overflowing with azaleas, cyclamen.
Your cufflinks glow in the candlelight.

That man is sucking on that woman's fingers.
He strokes them across his short gray beard.
I hear her laugh.  She thrusts a bread stick
into his mouth.  He sucks it, grabs
her hand, taps her knuckles, drums
on her knuckles.  His hair wisps
over his collar.  No tie.  Sneakers.
She is brown wool knit—trousers, sweater.

Do they see each other as young and fine,
ignore the limp thick lips, the jowly pallor?

But the young all look alike.
Only the old are recognizeable.

You order two kirs royale.

## Calypso

from Homer, *The Odyssey*, Book V, Robert Fagles translation

Seven years he lived with me,
sat at my table heaped with ambrosia,
eating my pomegranates,
drinking my deep-red nectar.

Each night he would enter my fragrant cavern,
its mouth ringed by vines,
clusters of grapes bursting ripe;
would climb into my flawless bed.
I am ageless, sea-nymph forever lustrous,
and he is son of Laertes and the gods of old.
I prefer him to any god I have ever known.

All day he would sit on the beach,
stare out at the wine-dark sea.
He yearned for his wife.
She is younger but mortal.
He yearns for her.

Seven years he lived with me,
eating my pomegranates.
Each night he would climb into my flawless bed.

The Olympian gods are jealous;
the Fates hate me.
I cannot keep him.
He is not mine, he yearns for her.

I must help him leave.
In my gossamer gown I will build him a raft.
With wildflowers in my hair I will hand him the adze.
I will give him the huge sea cloak,
the wineskins, bronze and hordes of gold and robes—
more plunder than he could ever have won from Troy.

He is only mortal,
though son of Laertes and the gods of old.
I live in eternity, he lives in time.

Time shatters me. Time cannot heal me.
The Fates are right, the Fates are wrong.
They wrench away my Love.
My grapes and pomegranates wither.

## Mother Has Stopped Doing Her Sit-ups

Dad travels a lot.
I think he has a bimbo in Mobile.
Mother's stopped doing her sit-ups.
I ask her to go with me to the spa,
but she says she's too busy.
She cleans closets;
wets cotton balls in alcohol,
swipes at the spots around the door-pulls;
with a nail brush picks at the crud
on bottlecaps.

I think she's given up.
I think she had a lover,
a young one, blond,
and he got tired of waiting,
and got married.

I show her torso shots
Of bikini'd girls in *Vogue*.
She says, *I still look like that*
*Lying down.*

I say, *At the spa you might meet someone.*
She says, *I might not want him.*
She says, *I don't have time.*
*I've got to get this house in shape.*
*Dad likes it spiff.*

## Everything My Mother Taught Me, My Daughter Contradicts

Ellen, whose waist-length waves
are too pretty to be decent,
French-braided my hair;
said it isn't getting thin,
I haven't colored it too dark,
my ears are small and flat.

Ellen, an undulating size six,
said my kind of thin is in
but I dress too old,
took me shopping in the juniors department,
said the pink and white stripe is me.

Ellen, who can roller skate *en pointe*,
begs me to skate with her to Westport,
says she finds all her beaux there,
says I can pass for thirty-five,
says Dad won't know I'm gone.

Ellen, whom I raised to think for herself,
thinks I need a Lover
tall and blond
to take me dancing.

## Mother Won't Wear Walking Shoes

*He had patterns that had been cut through*
*like the windows of Saint Paul's in either shoe.*
                    —Chaucer, "The Miller's Tale"

Mother won't wear walking shoes.
Her topaz and ruby heels spike
in gratings, shred on brick sidewalks.
I show her Bally flats, Adidas;
she says, *Henry won't love me*
*shod like that.*
Her calves are matchsticks.
I point to wheelchairs.
She says, *I tuck under,*
*my legs are steel.*
She silicones amethyst suede platforms,
disdains my LL Bean boat shoes.
Her boots, laced high,
have patterns cut through like cathedral windows.
She says, *Henry told me,*
*Don't buy shoes without me.*
I say, *He's in London.*
She says, *He'll know.*
*He's buying me slippers*
*to sip champagne from.*

## Mother Won't Buy Polypropylene

Mother was invited skiing.
I tell her about polypropylene.
She calls it polygamy-ethylene-acetylene.
I give her a fuzzy blue earband,
loan her my black hood.
She says, *I'll look like a terrorist.*
I send her out for a parka.
*You can't ski in mink*, I say.
*What would Catherine Deneuve wear?* she asks.
She insists the geese in my down coat are dead.
She comes back with a yellow cashmere sweater.
*On sale it cost about the same as polyethylene*, she says.
*Those Tibetan goats are still alive*, she says.
I send her out for jerseys and long johns.
She comes back with a gold jacket.
*I'm old enough for gold lamé.*
I ask, *Where will you wear it?*
She says, *It brightens up my apartment.*
*I might ask some people over.*
*I can wear it to the movies.*

## Mother Does Not Know She's Old

Mother was a bank officer. She wore
tailored English suits, navy blue
or black; pastel silk shirts, butterfly bows,
great-grandfather's gold cufflinks, pearl brooches.
She was traditional, predictable. I felt safe.
This spring she retired, gave me her banker's clothes.

This spring she burst into Florida colors, harem
colors, everything vibrant, iridescent.
Some days she channels young Miss Phryne Fisher,
that svelte detective from 1929 Melbourne:
all long floaty skirts and marabou-trimmed dusters.
Some days it's Twiggy mini skirts, little
flippy pleats, tiny tight t-shirts.

She cinches in her waist with bright silk
obis, encases her hips in spandex, flattens
her curves with cotton sports bras. She gave
me her Victoria's Secret push-ups and lace panties.

She lurches and wobbles on tiptoe on 1950s
springolator baby-doll platforms. She gave
me her Ferragamo pumps. For her daily walks
she wears gold or silver sandals.

Her makeup is Elizabeth Taylor-Cleopatra:
eyes outlined in kohl, lashes clumped thick.
Her hair, now auburn, a pert bob with bangs.

Her old friends do yoga, play bridge, wear jogging suits,
sneakers; their hair grows out to soft white ringlets.
Overblouses conceal their lost waistlines.

She flutters her clumpy eyelashes at the produce man.
He always gives her a hug. She could be his grandmother.
She flutters her clumpy eyelashes at the yard man.
She offers him iced tea. He stares back.
She could be his mother. She is so happy, I hate
to cross her. I must warn my ex-husband.

## No One Must Hear

Aya remembers, her nurse wonders

Each evening Aya inks numbers on her wrist;
each morning I scrub them off,
massage perfumed lotion.
I hold her hands, whisper,
*Aya, you are so pretty*
*your skin is soft and firm.*
*Which blouse will you wear today?*
She snorts,
>           *I don't like that one:*
>           *that girl who brought it*
>           *says she is my daughter,*
>           *but my daughter is dead.*
>           *She died in the train.*

No one must hear her say,
>           *Come My Darling, come to me,*
>           *there's time for more, once more*
>           *before you leave.*

He left to watch the comet,
to hear the dove clack and flutter
and disappear before she saw it,
before he flew into the plane
a red stripe against thick mist.

No one must see him slide his hand
along my back and change our skin to satin.
When I scream, I imagine rooms
of relatives, drifting, circling.

>           *No one must know,*
>           *no one must hear.*

>           *How can they know?*
>           *What can we know?*

The plane was landing
in driving rain and fog,
coming in low slow

coming in steep fast
dropping, levelling
toward the runway
plunging into the swamp,
auguring into the mountain
boring into, diving through
cratering the swamp,
denting the mountain;
the muck swallowed it,
the mountain cracked.

*No one must know.*
*No one must hear.*

All the clouds were in the valley;
the climbers never saw the storm.
Alligators, Bedouins, Sherpas:
they all patrol. They know
where the remains are.
Swamps, mountains, close up.

*We don't know.*
*One can't know.*

Her windows shut out sounds
of airplanes. The waited
thunderstorm is still travelling
across Kansas. The boy who flew
from the jeep to smash
the rock wall is cleaned off,

Bach and the newly baptized have gone home,
our bones float in grateful fatigue.

*How can they know?*
*We don't know,*

*one can't know.*
*What can we know?*

Voluptuous in red brocade,
Aya combs her Titian hair.
A thin person, glowing green
like toothpaste, celadon,
creaks up the stairs,
crunches like Styrofoam.  Skeletal.
She hears horses in the hallway.

At her table are eleven insane people.
They make bathroom noises.
When she closes her eyes to escape,
she sees a blue light,
the white tablecloth.

> *My husband was a soldier.*
> *My lover was a pilot*

> *No one must know.*
> *No one must hear.*

> *We don't know.*
> *What can we know?*

## I Can't Believe I Did That

I can't believe I did that,
and if you mention it, I will say I didn't:
*I don't know what you are talking about,*
*I don't remember,*
*I never.*

Still, I wonder: how did you find out?
Who could have told you?
No one saw us, I'm sure of that.
And *he* would never have said anything,
and of course *I* didn't.
Though, looking back now,
I'm pretty proud that I had the nerve.

He was much younger,
but just about right for me,
and I still had my looks
and everything, you know.

> The sky was calm, just a few floaty clouds,
> no moon yet
> so the far back corner of the garden
> was pretty dark and the hedges were high
> and overgrown so no one could see us
> back in the shadows.
> We took the champagne and two crystal flutes.
> I'm sure we were in love, at least I was,
> but we were not Ilse and Rick, and it was not Paris,
> and my husband was not Victor Lazlo
> and it was not tragic.
> Still, we were daring and stupid,
> rather like Icarus, but of course there was no sun,
> and no moon either,
> and we did not get caught and we did not die.

It was sublime.
But it did not happen and I don't remember
and I don't know what you are talking about.

*Appassionata*

Beethoven *Piano Sonata 23 in F minor, Op. 57, 1804-5.*
Jack Gibbons, Holywell Concert Room, Oxford, 10 July 2019

I.
Not from the waterfall, not from the wind;
not from the center of the burning bush—
  From the piano, the loud piano,
  pulsating in this crowded stuffy hall,
  baroque organ's golden pipes
  tall against flat white walls.

Here I could have felt my only love—
so far away in another country—
breathe into my ear, ruffle my hair.

Now I have known my True Love
(and another and another)
pulsing, writhing.
And I know the price of all that.

It is better now that the piano is not the waterfall,
or the roiling sea, or even the voice of God.
Galloping horses—yes—All Right.

  Slow, lyrical,
tinkling stream
  tapping high and low, faster: two melodies;
  back to the beginning fast slow hot cold pounding,
Yes: I give I give—
I give in.

II.
We dance across the breeze-green meadow,
rest by the cedar tree.
You touch my hair, you take my hand,
pull me after you into the forest.

We see a deer, it disappears
  First melody, soft, then pounding
You clutch at me—I am afraid
  First melody

114

I relax
        Pounding
I want to go back to the meadow.
You pull
        First melody – louder pulsing tapping
        First melody gentle
This is how I like you, how I first smiled.
But you start pounding, pulling me further
into the forest.  Quiet, dark, a stream
        First melody
Sunlight on the stream
        Melody harsh
I can't see the light from the meadow far away.
The water --the water -- rushes over stones,
we sit on a flat rock beside the stream.


III.
No.  You grab at my shoulder
        First melody too fast
No. Take me back
        First melody
I am confused. I like dislike.


Go deeper into forest. You are tender,
I relax, I trust
        Slow strong gentle
Yes I will go
        Underneath the soft notes
You are harsh but I am not afraid.  Yes I will go.


You touch my hair, I touch your wrist.
Your hands rough, voice soft.
You tap your fingers along my cheek,
we lie on the ground beside the brook.
I am not afraid, watch the sunlight
glare off the pine needles high above.
You are tired, I am sleepy.
        Soft melody, first or second – I forget;
I close my eyes and float away, it all floats away.
        The piano sounds like tin, the pianist is sleepy.

IV.
No.  Away.  The brook leaps up,
the deer returns to dance.
I am confused, what is happening?
      Notes so fast
Deer speeds up.
Do I see a fountain in the water?
Where is the palace? We should be getting back.
Where is my shawl? Where are my hairpins?
We have been here too long.
I am bored hungry tired. Let's go back.

Stop. It is getting dark.
Yellow eyes gleaming deep in the forest:
what is watching us?
Things are running around.
I stand still, my back against a willow tree.
      Slow fast
Can we go back now? I am bored, afraid.
What do you want from me? Let me go.

I can get back by myself.
I can run.
I hear horses.
Someone will find us.
Why don't they find us?
Let me go Let me go

## Matisse's Chair

If I were Matisse I would paint this scene.  I'd first
sketch in the Italian cloister, English garden—
ivy and field flowers—roses, delphinia;
outline the iron chair, swoop up the curving

back, spiral down the arms, curl,
now stop at each c-curve, feather the lacy
seat, splay down the twisting legs. Then
the woman.  All in black.  Lacy décolletage.

Thin, not bony, curvy under her clothes.
One arm she drapes across the chair back; the other,
down and off to her side, keeps her cigarette
low.  The air is green and dark.  It has rained

and will again.  The heavy tendrils rise,
take form.  She watches: like a rococo
*ébéniste* planning his boiserie,
like François Boucher painting Mme. de Pompadour's

pink silk dress, like Boettger shaping his Meissen
plates and figurines, like Vigée
Le Brun arranging Marie Antoinette's hair.
Trumpet vines spill over the arbor, shelter

her; but for the sounds of horns and motors,
she could be deep in the forest of Marly.  She
could be thinking of all her lovers.  The young
ones with the soft white skin and the minds like Aristotle.

The silent ones with the bodies like mortal sin.
The married ones who understood her.  All
of them far away and taciturn.  She wants
a new one: to grab her cigarette and stomp
it out, to take her hand and laugh with her
through the rain, to dance with her.

Were I Matisse, my brush would swirl black iron chair,
white smoke, pink and blue field flowers.  I would turn to her,
converse with her, be her Aristotle and sinner. And we live in the Louvre,
in postcards and parasols, dance down Paris streets and around our own meadow,
across water sparkling like confetti, through color exploding like popcorn.

# Notes

"Queen Nefertari's Knees"

"Knees of Mummy of Nefertari?" New Kingdom, Dynasty 18-20, 1539-1076 BCE. *Queen Nefertari: Eternal Egypt*, Nelson-Atkins Museum of Art, Kansas City, Missouri, 15 November 2019-29 March 2020

"Ice Age Bone Circle"

A.E. Dudin, photo. Nicholas St. Fleur, "Building with Bones: An Ancient Structure Mammoth in More Ways than One," *The New York Times,* 24 March 2020, p. D2. Discovered in a layer of volcanic ash brought to the Russian plain from Italy over 38,000 years ago is a forty-foot wide circular structure made from skulls, skeletons, and tusks of more than sixty wooly mammoths. Across Eastern Europe, archaeologists have unearthed about seventy such Paleolithic structures.

"Zippi Was Tall and Blond"

"Lovers in Auschwitz, Reunited," *The New York Times*, Sunday, 8 December 2019, pp. 30-31.

"Laocoön's Scream"

Section II, stanza 1: Virgil, *The Aeneid* II: 274-302, trans. Fitzgerald.
Section II, stanza 2: *Wikipedia*, "Laocoön."

"Lilies"

Nonce sonnet written in *Response to Above and Beneath the Skin, A Retrospective Exhibition of the Works of Petah Coyne,* Organized by the Albright-Knox Art Gallery in Buffalo, New York; At the Kemper Museum of Contemporary Art, Kansas City, Missouri, 16 September through 27 November 2005. Petah Coyne tells of an old Irish funeral custom of laying out the beloved in the parlor and covering the body with a blanket of flowers; as the flowers decayed, the family would add more and more flowers; eventually there would be a putrid mess. To memorialize and transform this custom, Coyne constructs sculptures from masses of stuffed birds and silk flowers that she covers with some two dozen layers of black or white wax. In some of her sculptures she hides the face and praying hands of a plastic Madonna.

"Will You Brush My Hair?"

Variation on a scene from Paula Vogel's play *Indecent*, after Sholem Asch's *God of Vengeance.* Echo of Daphne du Maurier's *Rebecca.*

## Acknowledgments

The characters in this collection are confused; they can't get it right. Mothers and children, lovers, soldiers: guardedly optimistic, because today is warmer than yesterday, they struggle with the ambiguity of love, death, regret.  But the book is not a downer: there are still yellow roses, mermaids, and a bit of tra-la-la in the forest. Thank you to the following publications where many of the poems in the book first appeared:

*Connecticut Review*: "No One Must Hear"
*Cottonwood*: "Perhaps a Ruined Abbey"
*Dimensions: Newsletter of the Thomas More Center for the Study of Catholic Thought and Culture*, Rockhurst University: "God is in All Sparkly Things," "Who Walks in my Garden in July?" "Caitlin's Angel"
*I-70 Review*: "Ashes Ruffle in the Breeze," "Drink," "Queen Nefertari's Knees"
*Kansas City Outloud II: 32 Contemporary Area Poets* (BkMk Press): "Mother has Stopped doing her Sit-Ups"
*New Letters*: "Mother Won't Wear Walking Shoes"
*Poets at Large: 25 Poets in 25 Homes* (Helicon Nine Editions): "Rice"
*Potpourri*: "At that Moment"
*Pushcart Prize XLVI*: "Mother Won't Buy Polypropylene"
*Rockhurst Magazine*: "As the Firefly Passes through Flame"
*Rockhurst Review*:  "Calypso," "Dancing Lady at the Luggage Repair" "Everything My Mother Taught Me, My Daughter Contradicts," "Golden Morning," "Mahakala," "Matisse's Chair," "Mother Has Stopped Doing her Sit-ups," "Mother Won't Buy Polypropylene"
*Can You Smell the Rain?* (BkMk Press):  "Mother is Dying," "Mother Is Scrubbing Her Floors," "Mother Mourns," "Mother Remembers Flowers," "Mother Won't Buy Polypropylene," "Mother Won't Wear Walking Shoes"
*Somewhere Between KC/MO and East St. Lou: an Anthology of Missouri Poets* (Spartan Press): "As the Firefly Passes through Flame," "At that Moment," "Budapest Street Scene," "I Ask the Little Prince about Yellow Roses," "Lilies," "Mother Won't Buy Polypropylene," "Mother Won't Wear Walking Shoes," "Rice"
*The Shining Years: Poems about Aging* (Blue Wild Indigo Productions):  "Mother Is Dying"
*Starting a Swan Dive* (BkMk Press): "Everything my Mother Taught Me, My Daughter Contradicts," "Mother Won't Wear Walking Shoes"

Many people have made this book possible. I am especially grateful to my editor Ben Furnish who wisely and graciously nurtured every word. The Diversifiers — Pat Lawson, Phyllis Becker, Eve Ott, Kathy Allen, Carl Bettis, and Gloria Vando — encouraged my writing process. My siblings – Cathy, Joanie, and John Cleary

— and my friends Bill Schwartz, Dan Martin, Rita Shelton, and Louis Oldani, S.J. read early drafts. My mentors Jim Engell and Desmond Egan expanded my horizon. I appreciate the editors of the journals who have previously published many of these poems, most notably at *I-70 Review* —Maryfrances Wagner, Greg Field, Gary Lechliter; Robert Stewart at *New Letters*; Bill Henderson at Pushcart; and Jason Ryberg at Spartan Press.

Patricia Cleary Miller is a professor emerita of English at Rockhurst University, where she founded and edited the *Rockhurst Review*. At Rockhurst she served variously on the executive committee of the faculty general assembly and as chair of the Department of English and of the Humanities Division. Her first collection of poetry, *Starting a Swan Dive,* won Rockhurst's Daniel E. Brenner Award for Scholarly Achievement. Her collection *Can You Smell the Rain?* won the James McKenna Award from the Gerard Manley Hopkins Society and International Festival; the poem "Mother Won't Buy Polypropylene" won a Pushcart Prize. Her nonfiction *Westport: Missouri's Port of Many Returns* celebrated the sesquicentennial of the town that would become Kansas City. Her chapbook *Dresden* gave a child's actual view of the Allied bombing.

Her secondary school was the French Convent of Notre Dame de Sion. She holds degrees from Radcliffe College, the University of Missouri-Kansas City, and the University of Kansas. She held a postdoctoral fellowship in poetry at Radcliffe's Bunting Institute. Her collections *The Maori Never Age* and its second edition *Crimson Lights* include poems celebrating her eight years as poet laureate of Harvard University's alumni association. She is a founding board member of The Writer's Place; she served as president and won its Muse Award.